1

IB BUSINESS MANAGEMENT
Internal Assessment

IB BUSINESS MANAGEMENT

Internal Assessment

The Definitive Business Management [HL/SL] IA
Guide For the International Baccalaureate [IB] Diploma

Dr. Sophie Muscatelli

Zouev IB Publishing

Published 2025

Printed by Zouev IB Publishing

ISBN 978-1-7385371-8-1, paperback.

Acknowledgements

A big thank you to John Landrakis, Costis Liolios, Ruchi NP Singh and Arwa Al-Salaimeh for their advice and proofreading of my work.

To my students Ignace Noordover and Omar.

To Anthew Chong, Miriam Kanner and our anonymous students for letting us use their IAs in this book.

I primarily teach IB students for whom English is a second language. My goal in creating this guide was to make it helpful not only for those seeking support with their Internal Assessments (IA) but also for those who need guidance on using appropriate language in their IA.

Table of Contents

PART I
THE BUSINESS MANAGEMENT IA GUIDE

Key abbreviations

Meaning	Abbreviation
Theory, Tools and Technique	TTT
Supporting document	SD
Business Management Toolkit	BMT
Research Question	RQ

Introduction

Before we start, I want to make clear that there are no strict rules regarding the number of theories, tools, techniques (TTT), or layout that you must adhere to. Your teacher may have their own way of wanting the IA to look or what to include; if so, that's great!

Secondly, when reading this book, you may see things in the examples in section 2 that I have advised against. This doesn't mean that the IAs lost marks. One common confusion is that the IB penalizes or deducts marks for what is missing from the IA. No! Examiners follow a "positive marking" approach, aka it does not penalise. As such, marks are awarded based on what is in the response/work, and not what is missing from the response/work.

In the examples in section 2, I have tried to give a cross section of IAs including all four concepts, primary and secondary data, quantitative and qualitative research.

The Basics

The IA is 1800 words or more. It is the same for both SL and HL.

However, the percentages towards your final mark are different.

HL - 20%

SL - 30%

You must integrate ONE of the key concepts (creativity, ethics, sustainability and change). Thus, you should have determined the concept and the supporting documents before you start.

You can use a small or large business. I would choose a large company like McDonald's to make your life easier because it has more information available.

Provide a research question for the business research project. as a conceptual lens through which to analyse (more on that later)

It can be forward-looking (see sample five) or backward-looking. Not too wide focus, and not too narrow that you don't have enough to write about.

Base your research on primary and/or secondary research. Although primary research is more time-consuming and does not necessarily lead to a higher mark

A single organisation should be chosen.

Different organisations for IA and EE (No double dipping).

No double-barrelled questions. This is when a single question actually asks about two different things at once.

Students should familiarise themselves with the assessment criteria.

Organisation

Need help choosing an organisation? Try these suggestions:
- Pick a company you like or use their products most often, or you can find more data and information (think MNCs)
- Choose a company that is situated in an industry that you want to work in
- Find a company that underwent an external growth strategy or a scandal
- Has a company marketed itself as sustainable, but reports show the opposite?
- Here is a frank opinion, if Business Management is your SL or you have no intention of using Business Management at university, then just make your life easy; think of a big company (so a plethora of information out there), do a backwards facing IA, because there's no need to give yourself the hassle.

Useful Activities

1. Write a SWOT or STEEPLE on the organisation (solely for research purposes; as I say further down, examiners hate these BMTs).
2. What statistics about the organisation are out there? Try Statista, Whip Media
3. Check out the organisation's social media. What image are they trying to portray?
4. Think about the internal and external environment.
5. What products do they offer, and where would you position them in an Ansoff Matrix or BCG?

You never know; when researching these activities, you might stumble across something you can use in your IA!

Concepts

Creativity

What is creativity to you? Note your definition. The IB does not look for a textbook definition. It has to be a definition that fits with your IA.

We do know that creativity is about:
A company creates a new invention for the market OR iteration, whereby the company creates a change or improvement in an existing product
What words do you think of when it comes to creativity?

- Creativeness
- Imagination
- Inventiveness

Ethics

Ethics should be a moral code by which businesses try to abide by (we would hope!). What words come to mind when you think about ethics?

- Principles
- Norms
- Standards
- Morals
- Morality
- Values
- Ethos
- Beliefs

Sustainability

Businesses need to change and promote sustainability before it's too late. More customers are looking for sustainable companies when choosing a product. How, where and when can businesses be sustainable? Please note that the concept of sustainability in IB Business Management is about conserving resources in the long term and not maintaining the business in the long term.

- Circular
- Renewable
- Supportable

Change

Companies need to change and adapt in today's ever-changing world. Companies can find themselves out of business if you don't keep up with the times. Ask yourself, what type of change has the company undergone? Internal or external change.

- Adjustment
- Development
- Diversity
- Modification

Example of Conceptual links to Syllabus Units

1.3 Sustainability and CSR and/or Triple Bottom Line* (TBL). See Sample 6 for an example of a TBL in an IA

1.5 Change and external growth methods

2.3 Does leadership need creativity?

2.4 Ethics when recruiting staff

3.4 Ethics in Profit and Loss Accounts or generally in accounting

4.5 Creativity in Social Media Marketing

5.2 Sustainability in production methods

5.4 Reacting to change in location

5.8 Creativity in R&D

*You might be wondering what TBL is. Although it is not necessarily in the syllabus you can analyse sustainability from TBL. Stakeholder mapping is another tool that students ask me about, yes, it's not in your text book but you can use it in your IA to evaluate stakeholder interests and conflicts. See sample 7 for example of stakeholder mapping.

Useful Planning Sheet

Research question:	To what extent…. (forward facing) How significant will …. How probable will …..
Key concept:	
Name of organisation:	
Links to Theory *(add unit number, e.g. Unit 1.5 Growth and Evolution)*	
Business Management Tool Kit	
5 supporting documents (within three years)	

Simple IA Hacks to Get You Started

No 1: We've all seen the memes about IB and its love of "to what extent."

coming up with a knowledge
question in TOK:

TO WHAT
EXTENT

But really, you should start with "To what extent" because it shows that you will introduce a balanced argument. See sample one's RQ.

Titles to avoid: What if...? How can...? How did...? These question starters tend to be too general, leading to a descriptive IA. 'What if' it's too hypothetical.

IA sample 3 uses "How does" however if you read the IA the student is successful in making a clear reference to the contrasting information in their 5 SD which makes for an effective analysis and evaluation.

No 2: Time to be an IB examiner: tell me what is wrong with this title.

How did Tesla's marketing strategy successfully help maintain its market leadership?

As aforementioned, this question starter tends to be too general, leading to a descriptive IA. Secondly, marketing strategy—well, marketing—is all of unit 4. So be specific! Even the 7 Ps are too broad. As you can see from sample one the student has only selected the Ps that are relevant to the RQ; the more specific you are, the easier it is to write a well-written and developed argument.

Avoid words in your title such as successful, unsuccessful, or scandal because the examiner can answer your question without reading your IA. For example, how has Company X's recent scandal affected its *market share*? The word 'scandal' implies something negative, so we know market share was probably affected.

Moreover, market leadership is also too broad. Which market are you talking about? Tesla builds rockets, electric cars, and robots, to name a few.

Tips for Research Questions

- You do not need your concept in the title

- Link it to a specific unit in the Business Management Syllabus
- Can you include a year, a duration or a geographical area?

No 3: Referring to the Concept: 5 marks (out of 25) are available for identifying and appropriately integrating a relevant key concept. But these are easy marks. (Yes, there's such a thing in IB). Whether you are analysing creativity, ethics, sustainability, or change, you MUST mention your concept:

- In the introduction (1 mark).
- In the body (3 marks). Ideally, in every mini-conclusion drawn from the TTT used and presented
- In the conclusion (1 mark).

TOP TIP: Make it easier for your examiner to see your concept and put the word in **bold**. See sample three for an example for how easy it is for the examiner to see the word if it is in bold.

When it comes to the integration of the key concept throughout your IA for five marks, the mark scheme asks you to:

Effectively integrates the analysis of the connection between the key concept and the organisation under study throughout the internal assessment

See the examples below on how (and how not) to be fluid and streamlined when mentioning your concept.

Not integrated well:

Change *is defined in the IB as an internal or external force that causes a company to change. That is what happened when Microsoft bought Activision Blizzard (2022).*

Integrated well:

*In 2022, Microsoft acquired Activision Blizzard due to **changes** in the gaming industry, which saw the rise of the Metaverse and cloud gaming.*

No 4: Before doing primary research, ask yourself… Are you sure what you want to learn isn't already available? Does it add value to your research? Could it complement your secondary research?

IB examiners can be strict about primary research results. They will wonder if your results are generalisable. Have the results been fabricated? If you are studying a small company with few employees, then primary can be used. I would avoid primary research if you are studying large companies; interviewing one employee out of thousands won't add anything to your research.

No 5: Using Synonyms: When it comes to your chosen concept—let's take ethics, for example—if you search this word in a thesaurus, you can find the following synonyms: morals, ethos, and honesty. Use a list of synonyms or related words throughout your main body. This shows you've understood and can conceptualise the concept in your written work.

No 6: BMT: Before starting, which of the 8 SL tools and 15 tools (described in detail further down) for HL can be used meaningfully to address your research question? Please note that you do NOT have to incorporate a BMT if it does not fit. Yes, you read that right.

Of course, BMTs are a useful starting point when researching your organisation and you may be worried to not include one, but keep the following phrase in mind: *Love is like a fart. If you have to force it, it's probably s**t.* Exchange *Love* for *BMT* and well, you get what I mean.

No 7: Did you know that you can use a documentary or podcast interview for one of your supporting documents? Caution! The examiner will not watch your documentary, so be sure to transcribe the part of the documentary or podcast that you are using, including the minutes. The transcript will be 1 of your 5 supporting documents. The URL of the video goes into your bibliography. You can use Clipto to transcribe your YouTube videos.

No 8: How many supporting documents? The directions state 3-5 supporting documents, BUT I advise going for 5. Only 3 supporting documents will not give you enough substance for your IA and will significantly impact your marks. Over 5 supporting documents and the extra ones will be ignored and your score capped to 1.

No 9: What supporting documents should I use? Use a range of documents that give different arguments, POVs and opinions. **Only 5 pages from each SD.** It's a good idea to use 1 internal source e.g. company website or annual report, and 1 or more SDs that shows a counterargument.

No. 10: Critique! Remember that you're using secondary research, so you MUST critique your supporting documents. This is a two-sided argument and a significant part of criterion D. To receive full marks for this criterion, assumptions and limitations should be stated.

No 11: How to upload your supporting documents. Upload your supporting documents in PDFs, which will be uploaded separately from your IA. In your bibliography, the first 5 sources will be your supporting documents, and then you will continue with the rest of your sources. It is important to label each of the supporting documents, e.g., "Supporting Document" (See the chapter on supporting documents for an idea.)

No 12: Analysing descriptive statistics (BMT 7). I see many students just rewriting what the examiner can see from the graph, pie chart or statistical analysis. You need to interpret the results; this means finding the evidence for the figures. Such as: *In 2022, 95% of people said that they would not re-subscribe to Netflix **because of the price increase** (Forbes, 2023).* Other ways to analyse rather than describe what does the variance tell you, conduct comparisons, benchmark and weigh the performance against the industry.

No 13: Balanced argument. Find an internal and external sources for and against to be able to create a comprehensive balanced argument

Word Count

The following are not included in the word count.

- Acknowledgements.
- Contents page.
- Tables of statistical data.
- Diagrams or figures (e.g. perception maps, break-even charts, decision trees, and the product life cycle)
- Equations, formulae and calculations.
- Cash flow forecasts or statements, Economic growth rates, Inflation rates, Profit forecasts, Sales forecasts, Sales Revenue
- Supporting documents.
- Citations
- References (must be in the footnotes/endnotes).
- Bibliography.

** Please note that headings and subheadings, SWOT box and STEEPLE are included in the word count

Page numbers are mandatory

Examiners stop at 1800 words, so don't go over the word count!

What Not to Do

It seems counterintuitive, but let's start with what not to do. It is better to know which IA mistakes to avoid in the beginning than to find them out at the end.

1. Do not use TTT outside of the syllabus; that is for EE.
2. SDs are to be published within a maximum of 3 years prior to the submission of the work to the IB. 20th April for May cohorts. 20th October for November cohorts.
3. Don't use out of syllabus terminology
4. 6 BMTs are NOT recommended for the IA. These are:

SL/HL	HL
Decision Trees *Leave decision trees to torture you in paper 2, as it's unlikely you'll have the correct primary data!*	**Critical Path Analysis (CPA)** *CPA is a future planning tool (so pointless if you are doing a backwards-facing IA). Just like decision trees, you are unlikely to have all the planning (primary) data, which would question the tool's credibility.*
STEEPLE Analysis *This analysis will reduce your word count significantly as extensive detail, and citations are required.*	**Force Field Analysis (FFA)** *Many students doing forward-facing IAs choose this BMT because it helps them weigh the pros and cons of a future decision. However, the driving and restraining forces require a weighted scale (e.g. 1-5). These weights are subjective, need primary data and will differ between you and the CEO.*
SWOT analysis *Although SWOT analysis is excellent for helping you understand your company better, it is too general and subjective (what you think is a strength; others may see it as a weakness).*	**Gantt Charts** *Without access to accurate company information (primary), this will make your Gantt chart unrealistic and not very credible.*

What happens if you really want to use one of these tools? For example, it would be difficult to develop a proper FFA without access to primary data (there are also other tools that require primary data, see table).

That said, it is still possible for a student to get a 7 (20+) even if the FFA is not properly utilized, only IF there are other tools/theories that are well developed. Incorrectly used FFA may only impact Criterion C, D and E (see section on understanding the criterion). See sample five for the use of an FFA in a forward-facing IA.

See sample 7 for an idea on how you can use FFA and Decision Tree in an IA. This student used a microbusiness and interviewed its stakeholders. From the analysis of the data the student was able to create an FFA and Decision Tree. Please remember that it is easier to obtain primary data from smaller businesses. Creating a FFA or Decision Tree for McDonalds would be inappropriate as you do not have access to primary data from MNCs.

BMT

Selecting BMTs is not about choosing your favourite or the easiest. It's the right tool for the right job. Moreover, if a tool doesn't fit your RQ, you are not obliged to include one. Yes, you read that right; you are not required to use a BMT if it's not necessary. I know I am repeating what I wrote earlier but you may not have been paying attention! :P

- Use a BM theory instead; after all you are expected to use/present 2-4 theories.
- Another misconception is that you must use quantitative data. There is no requirement to use quantitative data if it is not necessary.
- You can have a fully qualitative IA, or a fully quantitative IA or mixed methods IA. For example, if you are examining profitability then yes of course we expect to see quantitative data. But if you are discussing HRM theories of motivation then quantitative data may not be applicable here.

1. SWOT analysis: Situational tool
2. Ansoff's matrix: Decision-making tool
3. STEEPLE analysis: Situational tool
4. Boston Consulting Group Matrix: Situational Tool-Decision-making tool
5. Business plan: A planning tool
6. Decision trees: Decision-making tool
7. Descriptive statistics: Decision-making tool
8. Circular business models: Decision-making tool
9. Gantt charts (HL only): Planning tool
10. Porter's generic strategies (HL only): Decision-making tool
11. Hofstede's cultural dimensions (HL only): Situational tool

12. Force field analysis (HL only): Situational and decision-making tool
13. Critical path analysis (HL only): Planning tool
14. Contribution (analysis) (HL only): Decision-making tool
15. Simple linear regression (HL only): Decision-making tool

Design and create your BMTs rather than copy and paste them ("ready-made"). Examiners hate copy and pasted BMTs. Plus, you should fill in the matrices with information for maximum marks on Criterion C. Remember that information should be cited. You should make your BMT's context (aka country specific) unless you have chosen to look at a global phenomenon.

See my design for McDonalds below:

Ansoff Matrix

Market Penetration - Selling more in existing Markets Happy Meal Drive-Thru Big Mac (McDonald's annual report 2023)	Product Development - Selling New Products in Existing Markets Black and White Burgers (China) Freddo Espresso (Greece) Think anything from McDonald's cultural menu (McDonald's, 2024)
Market Development - Focuses on selling existing products into new markets. Planning outlets in Armenia (Smith, 2019)	Diversification - New Products in New Markets My Sneakers – Spain (McDonald's, 2024) CosMac Drive-Thru – USA (Anderson, 2023)

Figure 1: Ansoff Matrix, Author's own

BCG Matrix in the UK

Stars - Products with high market growth and a high market share McDonald's Breakfast	Question Marks - Products with high market growth but a low market share. McCafé Products
Cash Cows - Products with low market growth but a high market share	Dogs- Products with low market growth and a low market share

Chicken burger	Snack Wrap

Figure 2: BCG Matrix, Author's own (all from supporting document 1)

Remember, if a matrix does not apply to your analysis, don't waste words discussing it. Simply, bullet point the information inside of the quadrants and underneath analyse the quadrant(s) that are most relevant to your RQ. See sample 2 and 3 for a good example of Ansoff Matrix analysis.

How to Critique BMTS

You should critique the BMT in your IA and external exams. Begin by explaining how your selected BMT will help you answer your RQ. For example, *the Ansoff Matrix will determine whether McDonald's product development strategy was profitable or high risk.*

After analysing the tool, you should also clearly identify the drawbacks and limitations of your chosen BMT. For example, *the Ansoff Matrix does not capture McDonald's external competitive environment.* This will mean high marks in criterion D.

Try to draw a mini conclusion after the implementation of the BMT and then try to link it:

a) To the RQ
b) To the key concept

What Theory Should I Include?

There is no mandatory number of theories you must use; however, it is recommended to include at least two or more. The focus should be on selecting appropriate theories that effectively address your research question and support the analysis.

The quality and relevance of the tools and theories are more important than the quantity. I often see students using 4 or 5 theories, but with 1800 words, there's no way the student has analysed and evaluated the theories in detail. You should aim to demonstrate critical thinking, a deep understanding of the subject matter, and the ability to apply theoretical concepts to your investigation.

Primary Research

Creating a small-scale research project questionnaire involves several key steps to ensure that the questions are clear, relevant, and capable of eliciting valuable data. You can use online survey makers such as Google Forms or Survey Monkey to extract and analyse the data in helpful bar or pie charts. You can decide if you want the questions to be closed-ended (quantitative), open-ended (qualitative), or a mixed approach (qualitative and quantitative). See sample 4 for an idea of how to analyse primary data.

How can I construct a **questionnaire** or **Interview**? Here's a guide to help you through the process:

Questionnaire

1. Define the Purpose and Objectives
   - Purpose: Clearly define what you want to achieve with your research.
   - Objectives: List specific objectives that your questionnaire aims to address.

2. Identify the Target Audience
   - Demographics: Determine the characteristics of your target audience (e.g., age, gender, occupation).
   - Sample Size: Decide on an appropriate sample size for your study.

3. Choose the Type of Questions
   - Closed-Ended Questions: Use these for quantitative data. These can include:
   - Multiple Choice: Respondents choose from a list of options.
   - Likert Scale: Respondents indicate their level of agreement or frequency (e.g., Strongly Agree to Strongly Disagree).
   - Ranking: Respondents rank items in order of preference.
   - Open-Ended Questions: Use these for qualitative data. These allow respondents to provide detailed answers in their own words.

4. Formulate Clear and Concise Questions
   - Clarity: Ensure that each question is easy to understand and jargon-free.
   - Brevity: Keep questions short and to the point.
   - Neutrality: Avoid leading questions that might bias the respondent's answers.

5. Organize the Questionnaire Logically
   - Introduction: Provide a brief introduction explaining the purpose of the survey and how the data will be used.
   - Grouping: Group related questions together in sections.
   - Flow: Arrange questions logically, typically from general to specific.

6. Pilot Test the Questionnaire
- Testing: Conduct a pilot test with a small group from your target audience.
- Feedback: Collect feedback on the clarity and relevance of the questions.
- Revisions: Revise the questionnaire based on the feedback received.

7. Distribute the Questionnaire
- Medium: Choose an appropriate medium for distribution (e.g., online survey, paper survey, interviews).
- Instructions: Provide clear instructions on how to complete and submit the questionnaire.

Interview

Interviewing the right people with different perspectives in the company can help you gather really meaningful data from first-hand experiences and be critical.

1. Before the interview:
- Question Types: Prepare open-ended questions to encourage detailed responses.
- Key Topics: Outline the main topics and subtopics to cover during the interview.
- Sequence: Arrange questions logically, starting with general questions and moving to specific ones.

2. Schedule and Arrange the Interviews
- Contact Participants: Reach out to potential participants to schedule the interview.
- Location: Choose a quiet and comfortable location for face-to-face interviews or ensure a stable internet connection for virtual interviews. Remember to be prompt.
- Duration: Inform participants of the expected interview duration (typically 30-60 minutes).

3. Conduct the Interview
- Introduction: Begin with a brief introduction explaining the purpose of the study, what IB and IA are, how to ensure confidentiality, and how to obtain informed consent.
- Active Listening: Listen carefully to responses, showing interest and understanding.
- Follow-up Questions: Use probing questions to gain deeper insights (e.g., "Can you tell me more about that?" or "Why do you think that is?").

- Recording: With permission, record the interview for accurate transcription and analysis. For online interviews, use Fathom, which records and transcribes the interviews for you.

3. Transcribe and Analyse the Data
  - Transcription: Transcribe the interview verbatim, noting any significant pauses, emotions, or emphasis.
  - Coding: Identify and label key themes, patterns, and categories in the data.
  - Thematic Analysis: Analyse the coded data to identify common themes and insights.

4. Report the Findings
  - Use Quotes: Include relevant quotes to illustrate key points and provide evidence for your analysis.
  - Draw Conclusions: Relate the findings to your research question and discuss their implications critically without being descriptive.

Critiquing Primary Research

You must make a clear and balanced argument throughout your IA regarding primary or secondary resources. Primary critiques could include the research needing to be more generalisable, sampling or untrue answers from the participants.

You should collect different viewpoints to help you develop a more balanced and substantiated argument.

Here's some useful vocabulary for critiquing primary research:

1. Validity: Refers to how accurately the research measures what it claims to measure.
  - The study's validity is questioned due to potential biases in the sampling method (or if you know the person they could be answering differently to impress you or give you answers that they think you need).

2. Bias: The presence of systematic errors or prejudice in data collection, analysis, or interpretation.
  - Selection bias may have influenced the findings, as the sample was not representative of the broader population.

3. Generalisability: The extent to which research findings can be applied to a larger population or different contexts.
  -The small sample size limits the generalizability of the results.

4. Ethical Considerations: The moral principles guiding the research, especially concerning the treatment of participants.

- The study raises ethical concerns due to the lack of informed consent. (But seriously please get consent, there are ready made consent forms available online that you can tweak, once the signature is obtained you can put the consent form in your appendix.

Critiquing Secondary Research

Critiquing secondary research for the IA involves evaluating the sources and data to ensure they are reliable, relevant, and appropriate for your study. You should aim to use credible sources such as *The Financial Times, The Economist* or data-gathering platforms such as *Statista*. No blogs! Blogs are just people's opinions. Of course, using the company's annual and sustainability (if applicable) report or websites are also credible.

The methodology section is included in your introduction; here, you can critique your secondary resources or your conclusion. For example, *although McDonald's annual report includes useful financial data, it is authored by the company and may be biased. The report may omit certain negative business practices*.

Keep this list in mind when critiquing secondary research:
- Potential bias
- Only 5 SDs can be used
- Lack of experience to interpret
- Only 1800 words
- Further investigation is needed
- Cite, cite and cite again
- Avoid circular writing e.g. Business **growth** is about **growth** in their prospective industry.

Here are some useful phrases for critiquing secondary research:

1. Source Reliability:
- The reliability of the sources is questionable because some of them are not from academic or well-known publications.
- The sources used are mostly credible and come from reliable publications, which supports the arguments presented.

2. Thoroughness:

- The research does not cover all the important aspects of the topic, leaving out some key theories that could have added more depth due to the limited word count.

3. Diversity of Sources:
- The assessment relies too much on a few sources, which may lead to a narrow perspective.

IA Format

- Title page
- Table of contents (Remember to update this at the end!)
- Introduction
- Main body
- Conclusion
- Bibliography
- Appendices: The 3 to 5 supporting documents are in PDF format (remember to highlight the parts you use in your IA).

IA Structure

Introduction

Approximately 150-200 Words

You should try to include the following:

1. Organisation and organisation background.
2. To establish the context, a summary of the current issue, problem, challenge, or dilemma being investigated is presented, along with why it is important.
3. Methodology
4. If the word count allows, you can also include the mission or vision statement of the company. You may use supplementary material for this information so as not to sacrifice one SD.

Helpful expressions:
First the essay/research project will identify..... and then will look at......

Following on from this argument, an analysis of .... will be provided in order to determine......

Finally, the essay/research project will focus on......

Finish by writing: "which leads to the following research question...."

What not to do in an introduction
- Answer your Research Question in your introduction!
- Mention your personal feelings/judgement towards the topic.
- Try to fit in all your research and resources.
- Use clichés (or common knowledge information).
- Address your reader.
- Include overly detailed background information.
- Use the pronoun 'I'

See the sample Introduction below:

To what extent has *Starbucks* met its 99% ethical coffee standards in its supply chain by 2024 (184 words)

Concept: Sustainability

Starbucks is an American coffeehouse chain and one of the world's most recognisable brands. Headquartered in Seattle, Washington, the company operates more than 35,000 stores across 80 countries, as of 2022 (Bondarenko & Petruzzello, 2024[1]).

*While the company has publicly expressed its dedication to achieving 99% ethically sourced coffee, concerns have arisen regarding its ability to consistently meet this goal (Smith, 2023) throughout its extensive global supply chain. This dilemma raises questions about transparency, accountability, and the effectiveness of Starbucks' **sustainability** initiatives.*

Methodology

---

[1] Please Note that I am using Havard referencing style. You must use the referencing style chosen by your school. If in doubt, ask your Business Management Teacher or DP coordinator.

*This paper aims to evaluate **to** what extent has Starbucks met its 99% ethical coffee standards in its supply chain by 2024 by analysing its sustainability initiatives through Triple Bottom Line (TBL) and its financial growth using ratio analysis between 2021 and 2024. Secondary resources, such as annual and sustainability reports along with reputable news reports (the Economist), will be used in order to outline how Starbucks is meeting its initiative clearly.*

For the methodology paragraph, you should include qualitative (e.g., news reports) and quantitative (e.g., financial reports) data. You should indicate the validity, reliability, and diversity of the supporting documents. Try to acknowledge any potential weaknesses or biases in the sources. For example, if they are internal sources, are they likely to report what is not going well?

Main Body

1300 – 1400 words

Titles for the main body can be:
- Main body
- Analysis and Discussion
- Main results, findings and analysis of findings
- Qualitative discussion…..Quantitative discussion. (Begin with qualitative analysis and move on to quantitative)

Try to include

- Appropriate headings and subheadings
- A presentation of the findings from the SDs, BMT, and/or business theories and their integration into the key concept.
- Mini-conclusions for each tool/theory
- Balanced and evaluative approach + assumptions + limitations

It is really important that at the end of each analysis of a tool or theory you have an evaluative paragraph where you discuss limitations of the TTT and link it back to the question.

See an example layout below for analysing TTT in the main body:

RQ: To what extent has competitive advantage contributed to Walmart's current market leadership position in the North American food and grocery industry?

Concept: Change

Introduction Paragraph

Porter's generic strategies are a framework that describes how a company can achieve competitive advantage in its industry **(Quick introduction of the tool).** *Porter's generic strategies will analyse Walmart's competitive advantage over its rivals' position in the North America food and grocery industry particularly* **cost leadership** *and* **differentiation**. **(why this tool will answer your RQ).**

(Paragraphs on cost leadership and differentiation analysing Porter's generic strategies against Walmart. All evidence should be cited. Internal and external SDs. Show a balanced argument where perhaps Walmart did not achieve leadership or differentiation).

Evaluative paragraph before moving on to the next TTT

However, while these strategies have undoubtedly contributed to Walmart's competitive advantage, Porter's framework has limitations when applied to the complex, dynamic environment of the food and grocery industry **(Limitation of the tool)**. *Furthermore, Porter's model does not fully account for the impact of technological advancements or* **changes** *in consumer behaviour, all of which are critical factors in Walmart's success. Thus, while Porter's strategies provide a useful lens for understanding Walmart's competitive positioning in its industry* **(Link back to the RQ)** *they may oversimplify the multifaceted nature of the company's market leadership.*

How to Write Paragraphs for the Main Body

Many people have identified that there are five key components in a successful paragraph, so you may have seen many different acronyms that help to remember these. Some are:

PEEL	TEEL	WHEEL	PETAL	STEAL
Point	Topic Sentence	What	Point	Statement
Explain	Explain	How	Explanation	Topic Elaboration

Evidence	Evidence	Explain	TTT	Evidence
Link	Link	Evidence	Analysis	Analysis
		Link	Link	Link

Example Paragraph for Main body (PEEL)

*(Point) According to Starbucks, by the end of 2022, they achieved 99% ethically sourced coffee through their Coffee and Farmer Equity (C.A.F.E.) Practices developed in partnership with Conservation International (Starbucks, 2023). **(Evidence)** These practices ensure that coffee is grown and processed in environmentally **(concept)** sustainable and socially responsible ways, emphasising worker rights, fair wages, and environmental stewardship (Conservation International, 2023). **(Explanation)** Despite this impressive achievement, challenges and criticisms exist, such as the effectiveness of certification processes and the ongoing need to support smallholder farmers in adapting to climate change (Global Coffee Platform, 2023). **(Link)** Therefore, while Starbucks has largely met its ethical coffee standards, continuous efforts are required to address the remaining issues and further improve the **(concept)** sustainability of its coffee supply chain.*

How to Analyse Ratios

You can use the layout below for any ratio analysis in Business Management. I have used profitability ratios (if using profitability ratios, you should include all three). See samples 1, 2, 3 and 6 on how they have set out their financial analysis.

Profitability Ratios (Introduce what the ratio is and why it will answer your RQ)

Profitability ratios give insight into company X's profit per dollar of sales after expenses are deducted. This shows how efficiently company X generates profit …

Gross Profit Margin (GPM)

GPM is a profitability ratio that measures company X's gross profit, which is expressed as a percentage of its sales revenue.

Formula

(Gross Profit / Sales Revenue) x 100

Worked example from 2023

(20,000/50,000) x 100 = 40%

	2020	2021	2022	2023
GPM	11%	25%	39%	40%

In 2023, for $100 generated by **company X**, $40 was generated as gross profit. Comparing the years 2020-2023, it can be seen…..

For fluctuations find out why and cite the evidence!!

Net Profit Margin

The profit margin measures **company X's** overall profit after all costs of production have been deducted as a percentage of its sales revenue.

Formula

(Profit before interest and tax / Sales revenue) × 100

Worked example from 2023

(5,000/50,000) x 100 = 10%

	2020	2021	2022	2023
NPM	16%	15.5%	15%	10%

In 2023, for $100 generated by **company X**, $10 was generated as Net Profit. Comparing the years 2020-2023, it can be seen…..

For fluctuations find out why and cite the evidence!!

Return on Capital Employed (ROCE)

ROCE measures Company X's efficiency and profitability in relation to its size

Formula

(Profit before interest and tax / Capital employed) × 100

Worked example from 2023

Capital Employed=$80,000−$20,000=$60,000

(5,000/60,000) x 100 = 8.33%

	2020	2021	2022	2023
ROCE	7.33%	9%	10%	8.33%

In 2023, for $100 generated by company X, $8.33 was generated. Comparing the years 2020-2023, it can be seen….

For fluctuations find out why and cite the evidence!!

You may want to include graphs of your findings, see sample 2.

Conclusion

Around 200 -250 words:

- No new data should be included.
- Summarise all mini conclusions from the previous sections.
- Restate the question
- Clearly answer the research question.
- Point out any issues that need further investigation.
- Mention parts of the research question that have not been fully answered and might need more exploration for better understanding and further investigation.
- No recommendations are needed.

Example Conclusion

In conclusion, this study asks **what extent has** *Starbucks* **met its 99% ethical coffee standards in its supply chain by 2024?** *It has comprehensively evaluated the company's adherence to* **sustainable** *sourcing through an analysis of its annual reports, sustainability initiatives, and TBL.*

The findings indicate that while Starbucks has made significant efforts towards achieving its ethical coffee standards goals, there are areas where improvements can be made. The company's commitment to **sustainability** *and fair-trade practices is evident, but challenges such as low wages persist when ensuring consistent adherence across its vast global supply chain.*

However, the conclusions derived from the analysis may be influenced by company biases or exaggerations from media sources. Moreover, in-depth research is needed to understand the full scope of Starbucks's global supply chain. Most information available was from internal sources, which may have been presented more positively than what is true.

How to Cite

Incorporate secondary resources effectively: Use secondary resources to support your arguments and provide evidence for your claims. Use direct quotes, paraphrasing, and summarising techniques to incorporate secondary resources' information effectively.

Cite your sources: Be sure to cite your secondary resources properly to avoid plagiarism. Use a citation style such as MLA, APA, or Chicago to provide proper attribution to your sources. Ask your teacher or DP coordinator what referencing style your school uses.

Remember, it's not just for text sources. Other resources include:
- Artistic materials/Letters/Tweets/Visual materials/Lectures/Broadcasts/Blogs/
- Audio materials/Interviews
- Maps/Advertisements/Graphics/Conversations/Charts/Photographs

Google Scholar Hack

Click the speech marks

Copy and paste your chosen citation

Bibliography

List your 3-5 SDs first and then the rest of your references in alphabetical order

Example Bibliography

Bibliography

Supporting documents

1. Smith, John. "Starbucks Corporation Annual Report 2022: Profit and Loss Account." Starbucks Corporation, 2022.

2. Starbucks Corporation. "Sustainability Initiatives: Ethical Coffee Sourcing." Starbucks Corporation, internal website, 2023. Accessed 02/03/2023.

3. Johnson, Lisa. "The Journey to Ethical Coffee: A Conversation with Starbucks Sustainability Officer." Sustainable Business Today Podcast, episode 45, 2023.

4.   Thompson, Mary. "Coffee Industry Trends and Ethical Sourcing Practices." Market Research Report, ABC Research Group, 2023.

5.   Brown, Emily, et al. "Assessing Starbucks' Commitment to Ethical Coffee: A Comparative Study." Journal of Business Ethics 42.4 (2023): 567-586.Other sources

Other Sources

1.   Claar, Victor V. "An analysis of Starbucks as a company and an international business." Journal of Leadership, Accountability and Ethics 12.1 (2015): 83-89.
2.   Enderle, Georges. "Starbucks' CSR strategies: Using corporate social responsibility to strengthen its competitive advantages." Journal of Applied Business and Economics 18.5 (2016): 67-78.
3.   Kim, Chanwook, and Jeongsuk Koh. "Investigating corporate social responsibility of Starbucks: Focusing on corporate governance and environmental and social reporting." Sustainability 11.13 (2019): 3693.
4.   Lin, Li-Min, and Christine Kuo-Hwa Wang. "Assessing Starbucks' social responsibility performance: An integrated analytic framework." International Journal of Hospitality Management 49 (2015): 69-79.
5.   Mohr, Alexa. "Starbucks: A case study examining power and culture via radical transparency and ethical sourcing." Journal of Business Ethics Education 17 (2020): 199-208.
6.   Park, Myeong-Cheol, and Weidong Xia. "Starbucks' corporate social responsibility in China: Corporate philosophy, employee engagement, and consumer behavior." International Journal of Marketing Studies 8.3 (2016): 85-95.
7.   Pietrzykowski, Tobias. "The politics of corporate social responsibility in the coffee industry." Globalizations 15.2 (2018): 209-225.
8.   Poole, Nancy. "Starbucks Ethical Sourcing of Coffee." Darden Business Publishing Cases (2016).
9.   Schupp, Sarah. "Starbucks and the Evolution of Ethical Sourcing." Kellogg School of Management Cases (2019).

Appendix

Before you ask….No, you cannot put a SWOT or STEEPLE in your appendix!

Your five supporting documents with the parts highlighted that you used in your IA. You may wish to include
- **Additional figures and tables, such** as additional charts, graphs, tables, or images that complement your findings.
- **Survey Instruments**: Copies of questionnaires, surveys, or interview protocols used in your research.

- **Additional Documentation**: Extra materials such as brochures, flyers, or technical documents referenced in the text.
- **Legal Documents**: Contracts, agreements, or other legal documents related to your project.
- **Transcripts**: Full transcripts of interviews, focus groups, or conversations analysed in your research.

Example

Supporting Document 1

Home > Eco Life

The H&M Greenwashing Scandal: Has Business Learned the Lesson?

Despite its claims, H&M ranked C (mediocre) on the just published Impakter Sustainability Index and is currently not sustainable; the Index analysts concluded that if the retail brand genuinely pursues the goals it has set for itself and reports transparently, it could become "greener"

by **Camilla Ponte** — February 27, 2023 in **Eco Life**, **Index**

Last summer, Quartz carried out an explosive investigation into H&M's claims that it was sustainable and accused the fast fashion brand of "greenwashing" — i.e., making false or misleading claims about their sustainability efforts, particularly through the use (or misuse) of the Higg Index, which is H&M sustainability certification system.

What does the Higgs index measure? Who is the Higg Index used by?

The Higg Index is an assessment tool devised to evaluate the environmental impact of a product throughout its lifecycle, from design to disposal.

As mentioned above, a Quartz investigation revealed that H&M's self-reported Higg Index scores were often inaccurate or inflated, and the company was not fully transparent about its environmental impact. It even sometimes reported the opposite of what the Higg Index indicated.

IA CRITERIA

There are **seven** assessment criteria for the business research project.

This is the most important section of the book, as there are many hidden details in the mark band descriptions. For example:

Criterion A: Integration of a key concept (5 marks)

Criterion A: To receive full marks, you should EFFECTIVELY integrate the analysis of the connection between the key concept and the organisation throughout the IA. Simply mentioning the concept in passing or not means losing marks in criterion A.

0	Either the work does not reach a standard described by the descriptors below or the key concept identified is neither change, creativity, ethics, nor sustainability.
1	The student demonstrates knowledge of the key concept.
2	The student describes the connection between the key concept and the organization under study.
3	The student analyses the connection between the key concept and the organization under study.

4	The student partially integrates the analysis of the connection between the key concept and the organization under study in the internal assessment.
5	The student effectively integrates the analysis of the connection between the key concept and the organization under study throughout the internal assessment.

Criterion B: Supporting documents (4 marks)

Criterion B: You will not get 4/4 if you present SDs with limited scope. They should represent a range of ideas, e.g., financial (quantitative), qualitative, 1 x internal, and please, please, please include 1 SD that shows a counter-argument. Play it safe and have 5 SDs.

0	The work does not reach a standard described by the descriptors below.
1	There are only one or two, or more than five, supporting documents or they are of marginal relevance.
2	There are three to five supporting documents that are generally relevant but some lack depth
3	There are three to five supporting documents that are relevant and sufficiently in-depth.
4	There are three to five supporting documents that are relevant, sufficiently in-depth and provide a range of ideas and views.

Criterion C: Selection and application of tools and theories (4 marks)

Criterion C: It's about choosing the right tool for the job. For top marks: The business management tools and theories are effectively selected and applied with clear relevance to the research question.

This means introducing your TTT and telling the examiner why it will answer your RQ. For example, *using an Ansoff Matrix will analyse McDonald's product portfolio and identify the growth strategies of McDonald's new coffee and beverages venture, CosMacs Drive-Thru.*

SL students may use HL tools and theories only if they are directly relevant to their research question; however, you won't get more marks because you used HL theory. Plus, it may raise questions about academic integrity.

0	The work does not reach a standard described by the descriptors below.
1	There is a limited selection and application of business management tools and theories **or** these business management tools and theories are not relevant to the research question.
2	There are some business management tools and theories selected and applied to the research question. Their relevance to the research question is superficial.
3	The business management tools and theories are adequately selected and applied to the research question. Their relevance to the research question is not always clear.
4	The business management tools and theories are effectively selected and applied with clear relevance to the research question.

Criterion D: Analysis and evaluation (5 marks)

You should not have paragraphs of text without citations; otherwise, it looks like your opinion. So, remember to cite your SDs and references. Make clear references to contrasting evaluations. Don't leave this for the conclusion (see the earlier section on how to write paragraphs for the IA).

Copy and paste your RQ into your document's header (you can delete it later if you like). This means you keep your RQ in sight. Ask yourself if you have answered your RQ with a mini conclusion at the end of each TTT.

0	The work does not reach a standard described by the descriptors below.
1	There is limited selection and use of data from the supporting documents with no analysis and evaluation of the research question.
2	The selection and use of data from the supporting documents is superficial, leading to limited analysis and evaluation of the research question.
3	The selection and use of data from the supporting documents is adequate with some analysis and evaluation of the research question.
4	The selection and use of data from the supporting documents is sufficient, leading to a mostly effective analysis and evaluation of the research question with some integration of ideas.
5	The selection and use of data from the supporting documents is effective, leading to a thorough analysis and evaluation of the research question. There is a sustained integration of ideas with consideration of the assumptions underpinning the arguments and implications.

Criterion E: Conclusions (3 marks)

Have you matched your conclusion with what you analysed in the main body? Copy and paste your RQ into the conclusion and answer it. Make sure you also mention your concept again. What were the limitations of your research? Was there not enough information? Potential bias? Could not access company financial records? It does not mean your IA is weak because of limitations; even PhD theses have limitations.

0	The work does not reach a standard described by the descriptors below.
1	Conclusions are inconsistent with the evidence presented, or conclusions are superficial.
2	Some conclusions are consistent with the evidence presented.
3	Conclusions are consistent with the evidence presented and explicitly answer the research question.

Criterion F: Structure (2 marks)

Follow the layout presented in this book and this should help you structure your work.

0	The work does not reach a standard described by the descriptors below.
1	Limited structure.
2	Appropriate structure.

Criterion G: Presentation (2 marks)

Did you include the following required parts:

1. Title page
2. An accurate table of contents
3. Appropriate headings and subheadings
4. Numbered pages

0	The work does not reach a standard described by the descriptors below.
1	One or more of the required elements of a well-presented research project is missing.
2	All of the required elements of a well-presented research project are included.

PART II

SEVEN EXAMPLES OF EXCELLENT BUSINESS MANAGEMENT IA

The Internal Assessment featured in this section are all recently submitted IA that scored exceptionally well (band 7) after being moderated by the IBO. The IA are presented in the exact same way as they were submitted, without any edits or changes to formatting. We do not retain the copyright of these IA, nor is this publication endorsed by the IBO. The Internal Assessments are being re-printed with the permission of the original authors.

1. EXAMPLE ONE (23/25)

Research Question: To what extent did the collaboration with Travis Scott

Influence McDonald's brand image and sales?

Key concept: Creativity

Author: Simon K.

Session: May 2024

Level: HL

Marks Received: 23/25

Business and Management

Internal Assessment

Higher Level

Research question: To what extent did the collaboration with Travis Scott influence

McDonald's brand image and sales?

Key concept: Creativity

Word count: 1770

Session

Student number

Table of Contents

Introduction

McDonald's is one of the largest fast-food chains in the world, specializing in offering wide range of products, including burgers, fries, soft drinks, and more (Ganti, 2022). McDonald's has restaurants all over the world, and it has become a favorite among millions of customers. One of the key factors contributing to its remarkable success is its effective marketing approach which has played a significant role in establishing the brand's dominance in the industry (Petre, 2023).

In recent years, McDonald's undertook a strategic step by collaborating with influential figures from the world of music, sports, and entertainment to further increase its brand image and attract a broader customer base. One such notable collaboration was with Travis Scott, a globally recognized rapper. The unique partnership between McDonald's and influential figures challenged traditional ideas about brand partnerships and created excitement surrounding the potential collaborations between music and fast food. Thus, the collaboration highlighted McDonald's creative and innovative approach to marketing. By teaming up with a prominent figure in the music industry, McDonald's demonstrated its willingness to think outside the box.

Considering that the collaboration between Travis Scott and McDonalds was a unique and new marketing approach in the fast-food industry, the outcomes could range from success to potential setbacks. Consequently, the aim of this exploration is to examine how McDonald's creative marketing strategy, in form of collaboration with Travis Scott, influenced the company's brand image and sales. The brand image will be examined using qualitative business tool, 7Ps marketing. On the other hand, the effects of the collaboration on company's sales will be explored using quantitative business method, Financial Analysis. All analyses will be supported by secondary data to obtain wide range of perspectives. The supporting documents include articles representing audience's feedback and financial statement. Although they are valuable in providing diverse perspectives, the secondary sources are subject to bias, therefore, compromising their reliability.

Findings

The collaboration between Travis Scott and McDonald's aimed to create a unique and limited-time meal called the "Travis Scott Meal." The meal included some of Travis Scott's favorite McDonald's menu items, such as the "Travis Scott Quarter Ponder", medium fries with barbeque sauce and a medium Sprite[1]. Furthermore, as part of the collaboration, exclusive merchandise was produced. Limited-edition merchandise featuring co-branded designs was released which included clothing items and accessories featuring elements from both Travis Scott's brand and McDonald's logo (Snowden, 2020).

The partnership generated immense excitement among Travis Scott's fan base. McDonald's strategic decision to collaborate with Travis Scott was mainly influenced by the artist's cultural relevance, particularly among younger customers (Taylor, 2020). Consequently, McDonald's effectively demonstrated its adaptability and willingness to conform to contemporary trends.

Overall, the collaboration with Travis Scott played a significant role in reshaping McDonald's brand image, portraying it as a dynamic and culturally relevant brand that is willing to take risks and connect with consumers in unique and exciting ways[2].

---

[1] See Supporting Document 2.
[2] See Supporting Document 1.

Analysis of the findings

7Ps Marketing Mix

The 7 Ps model is a marketing strategy tool examining 7 main sectors that determine the success of services or products – these include Product, Promotion, Place, People, Process, and Physical evidence (Hanlon, 2023). By examining each sector, companies can gain insights into the strengths and weaknesses of their product marketing efforts. However, in this exploration, the sections Place, Price, Process and Physical Evidence will not be considered, because they are not directly relevant to the examination of the research question. It is important to acknowledge that the analyses are subjective, affecting the reliability of the findings.

Product

The partnership introduced a simple 6$ meal and a range of exclusive merchandise. The meal consists of Travis Scott's favorite food items from McDonald's. It is interesting to note that these menu choices have been a part of the artist's preferences since his childhood, reflecting a genuine and personal association with the brand[3].

Furthermore, the simplicity of the menu was a key factor that contributed to the success of the collaboration. While the collaboration introduced a unique and personalized meal, it was designed to resonate with a broad range of consumers by incorporating familiar and iconic McDonald's menu items[4].

Promotion

A significant factor contributing to the success of the collaboration was the clever implementation of a limited time offer for the products. This innovative approach played a crucial role in captivating consumers to try the unique Travis Scott meal and associated merchandise.

---

[3] See Supporting Document 1.
[4] See Supporting Document 3.

Moreover, the collaboration created a remarkable trend on Tik Tok, where individuals filmed themselves singing along to Travis Scott's songs in the drive-thru. The trend went viral, providing McDonald's with free publicity and increased brand recognition. The overwhelming success of the TikTok trend was so immense that it resulted in a shortage of supplies, serving as a clear indication of its overwhelming popularity and impact (Threadcraft, 2020).

People

It was evident from the beginning that the collaboration would attract a substantial audience, given the artist's extensive following, particularly on social media and music streaming platforms[5]. Travis Scott's outstanding following on Instagram, currently equal to 33.4 million, allowed for successful promotion of the McDonald's burger. Artist's multiple posts about the collaboration received around 10 million likes[6]. This shows how influential Travis Scott's social media presence is and how effectively the singer could reach and connect with devoted fans.

However, it is important to note that collaborations also come with potential risks. In the case of the partnership, one such challenge arose from Travis Scott's explicit and violent lyrics, which contradicted the family-friendly image that McDonald's strives to maintain (Taylor, 2020). This created a potential conflict between the Scott's artistic expression and the brand's reputation for being suitable for all audiences.

Overall, McDonald's collaboration with Travis Scott successfully utilized product innovation, strategic promotion, and the influence of a popular artist to enhance its brand image and attract a wider customer base. The introduction of a personalized meal, clever limited-time offers, and the effective marketing through social media platforms contributed to the collaboration's success. However, the partnership also presented challenges regarding the Travis Scott's artistic expression with McDonald's family-friendly image. Nonetheless, the collaboration effectively demonstrated McDonald's creative marketing approach and its ability to connect with consumers in unique and exciting ways.

---

[5] See Supporting Document 3.
[6] See Supporting Document 2.

Financial analysis

A quarterly analysis was conducted to assess the influence of the Travis Scott and McDonald's collaboration on sales. Since financial data specifically related to the collaboration was not readily available, the analysis focused on examining the sales performance of McDonald's during the quarters when the collaboration took place. The data was taken from a Macrotrends database[7]. By comparing the sales figures from those quarters, it was possible to observe any significant changes or trends that could be attributed to the collaboration. One limitation of using revenue data is its generality. The revenue figures include not only the impact of the collaboration but also other factors that may have influenced sales during the same period. As a result, it becomes challenging to examine the specific contribution of the collaboration to the revenue figures.

The collaboration took place between 8th September till 4th October in 2020 (Marain, 2020). Consequently, the revenues connected to the partnership come from 3rd and 4th quarter.

---

[7] See Supporting Document 4.

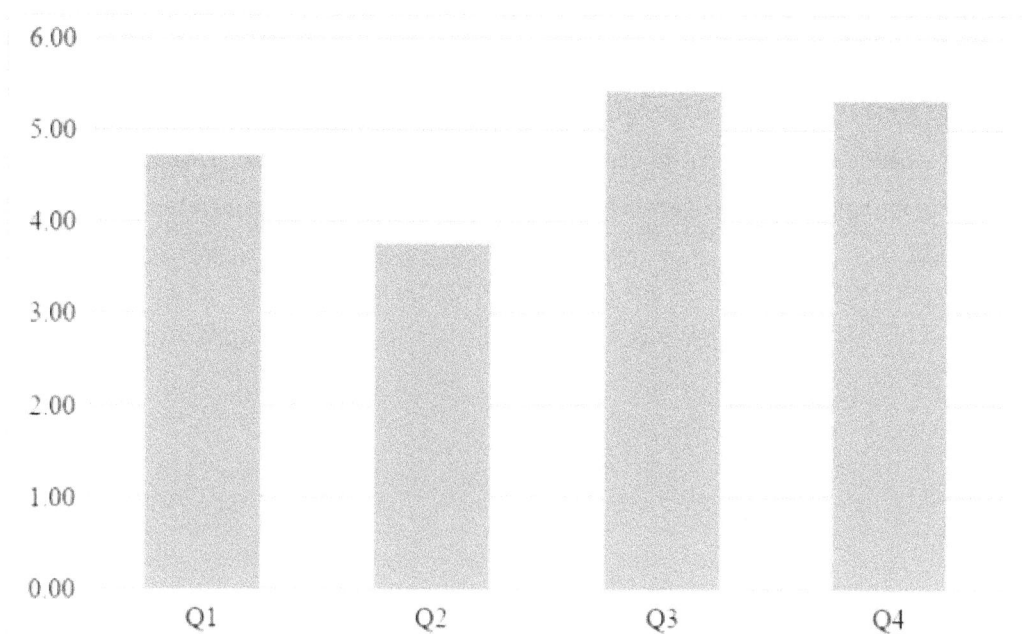

Figure 1. McDonald's quarterly revenues in 2020 (in million dollars)[8]

As seen on the graph, during the collaboration with Travis Scott in the third and fourth quarters, there was a noticeable impact on sales. In the first (Q1) and second quarter (Q2), revenue was recorded at $4.71 million and $3.76 million respectively. However, during the third quarter (Q3), when the collaboration took place, revenue increased to $5.42 billion. This signifies a positive influence on sales during the period of the collaboration. In the fourth quarter (Q4), revenue remained relatively high at $5.31 billion, indicating that the collaboration continued to have a positive effect on McDonald's sales. These revenue figures suggest that the partnership with Travis Scott contributed to increased customer spending and generated additional revenue for McDonald's during the collaboration period.

Additionally, it can be observed how the collaboration helped McDonalds during the decline in sales caused by the Covid-19 pandemic. According to Amelia Lucas and Kate Rogers, the partnership allowed McDonald's to achieve its highest monthly sales in September (which is in third quarter). The positive impact can be also observed in the quarterly analysis, where the third quarter recorded highest revenues.

---

[8] See Supporting Document 4.

Although reported revenues include factors beyond the collaboration, it is evident that the partnership between Travis Scott and McDonald's had a positive impact on the company's sales. McDonald's itself acknowledged the success of the collaboration by highlighting instances where supplies ran out in certain locations (Threadcraft, 2020). This serves as an indicator of the collaboration's overwhelming success and its influence on increasing sales for McDonald's.

Conclusion

The examination assisted with 7Ps Marketing Mix and Financial Analysis allowed to provide an answer to the research question: "To what extent did the collaboration with Travis Scott influence McDonald's brand image and sales?". The collaboration proved to be a successful marketing venture that positively impacted the company's brand image and sales. McDonald's demonstrated its innovative and creative approach to marketing by teaming up with Travis Scott, a globally recognized rapper. The collaboration introduced a unique and personalized meal, by incorporating Travis Scott's favorite McDonald's menu items. The clever implementation of a limited-time offer for the products and the creation of a viral trend on TikTok further enhanced the collaboration's success.

The qualitative analysis using the 7Ps marketing mix highlighted the strengths of the collaboration. The simplicity of the menu, the effective promotion through social media, and the overwhelming response from Travis Scott's extensive following contributed to the positive impact on sales. However, the partnership also presented challenges, such as the potential conflict between Travis Scott's explicit lyrics and McDonald's family-friendly image.

The financial analysis, though limited due to the lack of specific data on the collaboration, indicated an upward trend in revenue during the third and fourth quarters when the collaboration took place. This indicates a positive influence on sales during the collaboration period and suggests that the partnership contributed to increased generated revenue for McDonald's. The collaboration also helped McDonald's overcome the decline in sales caused by the COVID-19 pandemic.

In conclusion, the collaboration between Travis Scott and McDonald's successfully reshaped the brand image of McDonald's, portraying it as a dynamic and culturally relevant brand. The partnership demonstrated McDonald's willingness to take risks and connect with consumers in unique and exciting ways. To further validate the positive influence of the collaboration on the company's sales, the Return-on-Investment analysis would be appropriate measure. This will allow for direct assessment of McDonald's financial returns from the collaboration.

BIBLIOGRAPHY + APPENDICES OMITTED

2. EXAMPLE TWO (19/25)

Research Question: To what extent has Uber's acquisition of

Postmates increased its profitability?

Key concept: Change

Author: Ignace Noordover

Session: May 2024

Level: HL

Marks Received: 19/25

Business Management
Internal Assessment

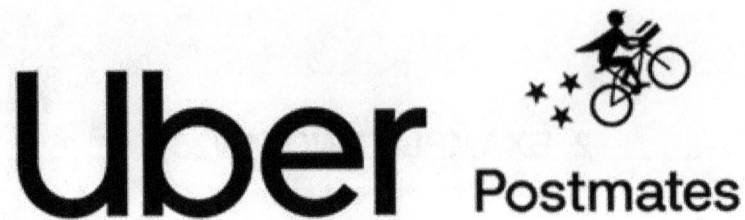

Research Question:

To what extent has Uber's acquisition of
Postmates increased its profitability?

Concept: Change
Word Count: 1,754
May 2024 Session

Table of Contents

Introduction

Launched in 2009, Uber Technologies Inc. is the world's most valuable startup, worth around $96 billion (Macrotrends, 2023), primarily providing ride-hailing services in addition to food delivery, package delivery, and freight transport around the world (Brittanica, 2023). Uber's food delivery service 'UberEats' proved successful being the company's second-largest stream of revenue, $2.5 Billion in 2019 (Trefis, 2020). With a 23% share of the American food delivery service market, Uber is second to Doordash[1] who holds a 44% market share, while Postmates won 8% of the market share (Forbes, 2020). Uber is now available in over 10,000 cities (Uber, 2023) and UberEats in 500 cities globally (UberEats, 2023).

Despite Uber being one of the most successful ride-sharing companies in the world with exponential growth since its inception, they are yet to be profitable. Since their first round of venture capital funding ($11 million raised), they have amassed over $25.2 billion in funding between 2011 and 2022 (Business Model Analyst, 2023). In 2019, Uber went public on the New York Stock Exchange and raised $8.1 billion in its initial public offering. Although, after reporting 7.6 billion trips and $31.9 billion in revenue at the end of the 2022 financial year, Uber still made a net loss of $9.1 billion (Investopedia, 2023). In efforts to increase market share and in turn profitability, Uber Technologies Inc. acquired Postmates Inc. in a $2.65 billion all-stock transaction in 2019 (Forbes, 2020).

Postmates Inc. was founded in 2011 and designed to deliver restaurant food in addition to groceries, electronics, liquor, and even pharmaceuticals in under an hour (Zippia, 2023). Their USP is that customers could order anything from virtually anywhere, as the restaurant (or store) doesn't need to be partnered with Postmates to be ordered from (gigworker, 2023). Despite their USP and quick delivery, Postmates never turned a positive net income. (LA Times, 2020).

---

[1] Doordash is a food delivery service in the United States of America

Issue Statement

Postmates was valued at $1.85 billion in early 2019 whereas Uber was valued at $120 billion before their IPO in mid-2019 (Investopedia, 2023). The horizontal acquisition of Postmates by Uber "provides more choice and convenience for consumers, new demand and tailored technology offerings for restaurants, and increased income opportunities for delivery people." (Postmates, 2020). Through this acquisition, Uber used different strategies to become more profitable.

Objective and Methodology

The objective of this paper is to evaluate how Uber's acquisition of Postmates will assist the company in becoming profitable by analyzing its growth strategies through the Ansoff Matrix and their financial growth using ratio analysis between 2018-2023. Ubers' market growth, financial statements, and synergies post-merger will be discussed using quantitative and qualitative data and research. This study will clearly outline how the growth strategies were used during the acquisition of Postmates and how this undertaken change helped bring Uber closer to profitability. However, the conclusions derived from the analysis may be influenced by the biases or exaggerations of the media sources.

Ansoff Matrix

The Ansoff Matrix is a strategic planning tool laid out in a two-by-two framework- of existing/new markets, and existing/new products- providing four strategies for growth. Each strategy has a varying level of risk involved (Strategies for Influence, 2019). Uber utilizes Product Development through their acquisition of Postmates whilst simultaneously also implementing market penetration to maintain and increase sales through this change to increase profitability.

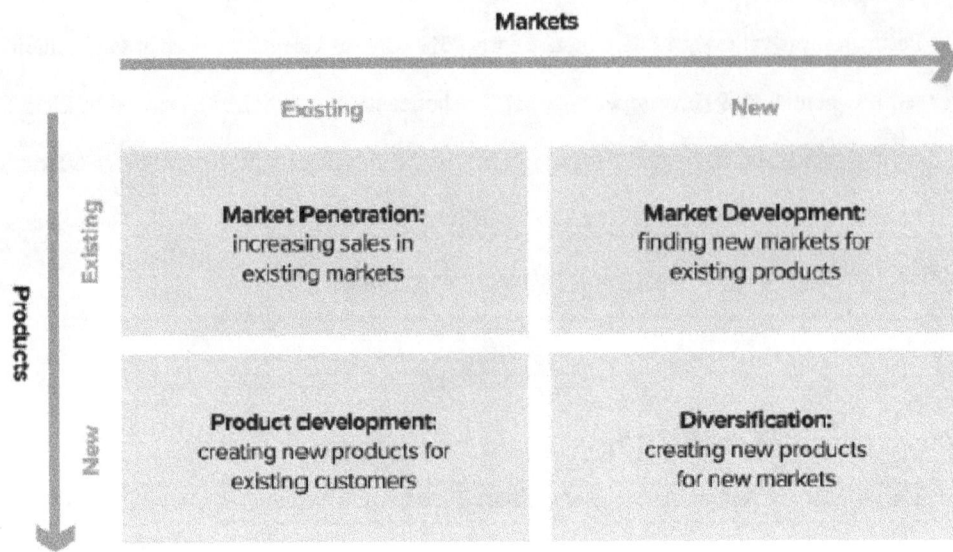

Markets

Existing | New

Products

Existing:
Market Penetration: increasing sales in existing markets

Market Development: finding new markets for existing products

New:
Product development: creating new products for existing customers

Diversification: creating new products for new markets

(Business Growth Hub, 2023)

Ratio Analysis

Ratio Analysis is made up of profitability, liquidity, and efficiency ratios that judge the financial performance of a business by analyzing its financial statements. The profitability ratios- gross profit margin (GPM), net profit margin (NPM), and return on capital employed (ROCE)- state the improved/worsened profits of Uber for multiple years (2018-2023) which will, in turn, answer how the acquisition of Postmates led to a **change** in profitability.

Research and Analysis of Change Using Ansof Matrix and Ratio Analysis

Product Development

USP: Grocery Delivery

One of Postmates USP's was it's grocery delivery services which signified their mission to allow anyone to get anything delivered on-demand (Tech Crunch, 2017). In 2019, 80% of Postmates' total deliveries were food orders, proving the grocery services' success (Dev Technosys, 2020). Hence after the acquisition, Uber was able to rapidly advance their food delivery R&D[3] as they could refer to Postmates' service' for the prototype and test marketing stage, resulting in an efficient and effective launch to their Grocery service on UberEats (Uber Newsroom, 2020). This was a medium-risk strategy as it involved bringing a new product to their existing consumers and market, where the service's success would directly influence the brand development of Uber (Business Management Textbook, 2022). Ubers new grocery delivery service had a high chance of success given the change brought about by the application and integration of Postmates technology and brand awareness surrounding their original service. The addition of Postmates technology brought positive **change** to Uber's grocery delivery service as it made it more successful.

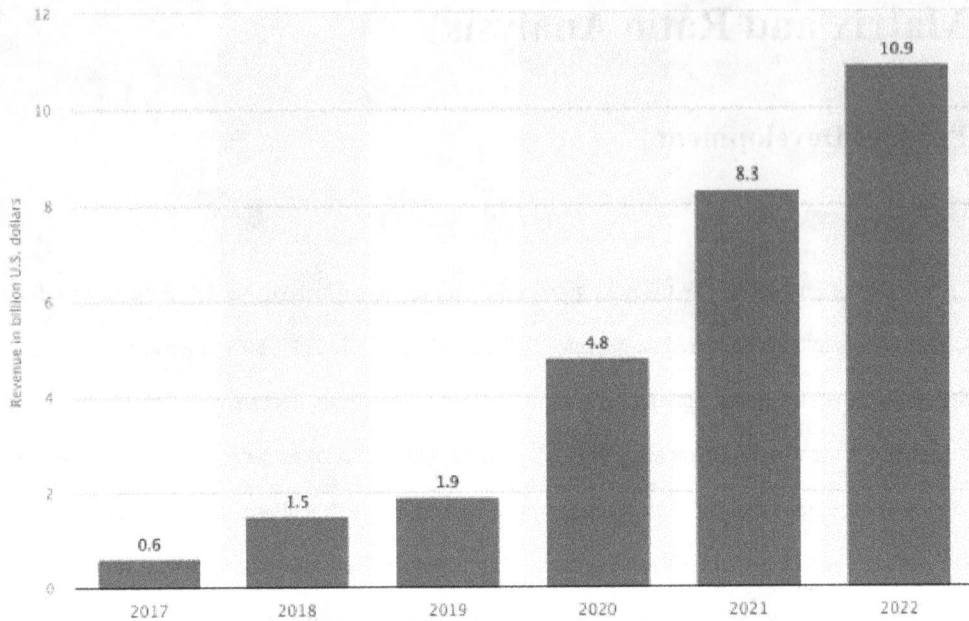

(Statistica, 2020)

The revenue of the Uber Eats app almost doubled from $4.8 to $8.3 billion between 2020 and 2021, when their grocery service was introduced. This increase in profit proved that Uber's product development strategy had been successful and in turn, helped the company in its goal to reach profitability.

Acquisition of Merchants

Postmates started in the early stages of food delivery and has since amassed over 600,000 restaurants on their platform (Nations Restaurant News, 2020). In comparison to Uber who had 500,000 merchant partners. Uber could not purchase from non-partnered restaurants like Postmates, they didn't have this feature due to the challenges they posed for Postmates and other companies. Therefore after the acquisition, Uber could deliver to non-partnered restaurants without the risk of damaging their own brand

68

image. As a result of this **change** in number of merchants, Uber provides more choice and convenience to their customers which means they could increase their profitability.

Market Penetration

Acquisition of Customers

There were over 110 million users of food delivery apps in the United States in 2020 (apps rhino, 2023). In this year, Postmates had 8.8 million users (Dev Technosys, 2023), and Uber Eats 66 million users (BusinessofApps, 2023). Resultingly, Uber gained 8.8 million users from their acquisition. Acquiring Postmates customers was a key **change**, as they reached different consumer groups and segments in the market.

The total revenue of the United States food delivery market in 2020 was $139.39 billion (Statistica, 2023). That same year, Postmates' revenue was $640 million (BusinessofApps, 2023) and Ubers' $4.8 billion. Therefore, following the acquisition, Uber's annual revenue increased to $5.42 billion from delivery services in 2020. In the following year, 2021, there was a 31.3% increase in revenue for Uber and 14.1% increase for Postmates equalling a total increase in annual revenue of $2.69 billion.

Uber Eats annual revenue 2017 to 2022 ($bn)	
Year	Revenue ($bn)
2017	0.6
2018	1.5
2019	1.9
2020	4.8
2021	8.3
2022	10.9
Sources: *Bloomberg*, *Company data*, *Food Delivery App Report*	

Postmates annual revenue 2014 to 2021 ($mm)	
Year	Revenue ($mm)
2014	8.6
2015	55
2016	135
2017	250
2018	400
2019	500
2020	640
2021	730
Sources: *Company data*, *Food Delivery App Report*, *TechCrunch*	

(BusinessofApps, 2023)   (BusinessofApps, 2023)

The Ansoff matrix tool was insightful and provided an accurate depiction of Uber's growth through the **changes** experienced when acquiring Postmates. However, the tool is limited as it doesn't take into account customer preferences and changes within/outside the market like environmental factors and/or monopolistic companies. Overall, the application of the ansoff matrix proved how the improved grocery delivery service and acquisition of merchants and customers from Postmates improved the profitability of Uber.

Ratio Analysis

Profitability

The gross profit margin ratio[2] (GPM) represents the value of a firm's gross profit as a percentage of its sales revenue. A GPM of 50-70% is considered healthy and indicates that the company is gaining a fair amount of profit from its sales revenue. Uber's gross profit oscillated at 50% from 2019 to 2021 and has come to a steady 40% for the past 3 years (2021-2023). This decline indicates their increased COGS[3] due to the increased R&D of their grocery and delivery services with the acquisition of Postmates' technology. This 50% GPM is further explained by the **change** in Uber's product mix as they started selling products through their grocery service meaning a larger amount of lower-margin products compared to before.

Gross Profit Margin (Quarterly)

(Macrotrends, 2023)

---

[2] GPM = Gross Profit/Sales x 100
[3] Cost of Goods Sold

The net profit margin ratio[4] (NPM) provides the percentage of sales revenue that a company keeps after accounting for their costs as well as taxes and interest. In other words, the higher the NPM the higher the profit margin of a company. The graph indicates that in FY19Q4 the NPM had dipped to -80% because of the Postmates acquisition, however, after that initial dip, their NPM rose back to a near-positive value indicating they almost became profitable. Although this was only a result of their divestitures, nevertheless, the overall improvement along the NPM curve indicates they have just become profitable in their last two quarters of FY23. Ubers growth strategies can be credited to its continuous growth since its acquisition and hence, proves the acquisition led to a **change** in profitability, and ultimately, profit in FY23.

Net Profit Margin (Quarterly)

(Macrotrends, 2023)

The return on capital employed[5] (ROCE) is the last profitability ratio, indicating how effectively Uber used their capital within a given period. In 2019 their ROCE was -37.5% indicating that they were in a lot of debt and couldn't cover their capital employed. This ROCE steadily increased from -37.5% to -5.9% in 2022 with a positive ROCE **change** in 2023 of 4.2%. Hence signifying how the company made a profit high enough to cover their capital which was probably a result of their increased revenue due to their expanded customer base and synergies by acquiring Postmates. This upward trend since the acquisition can mean the synergies of Postmates customers and technology led to Ubers improved ROCE and hence profitability.

---

[4] Profit before interest and tax/Sales revenue x 100
[5] Profit before interest and tax/Capital employed x 100 (capital employed = Total Assest - Total Liabilities)

Return on Capital Employed (ROCE)

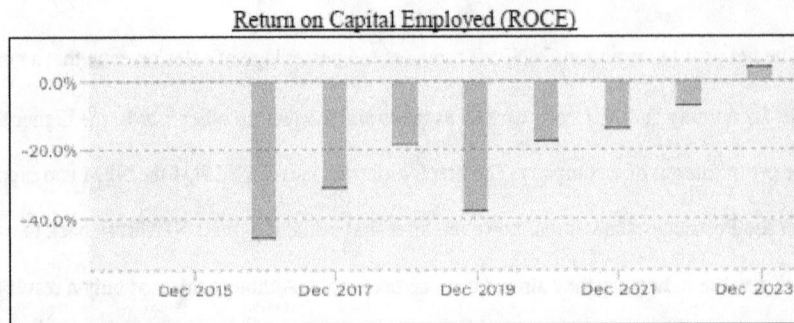

(Finbox, 2023)

Profitability ratios displayed Uber's financial response to the acquisition of Postmates. The GPM NPM, and ROCE provided the required information to conclude Ubers growth strategies were successful and its resulting increased profitability. However, the ratio analysis was limited as it isn't clear through the financial data how each contribution from the Postmates acquisition attributed to the ratios. Secondly, there was no comparison of ratios against competitors through benchmarking. Overall the profitability ratios provided a good indication of how Uber's profitability **changed** after they acquired Posmates.

Conclusion

Uber's acquisition of Postmates directed them toward profitability. The Ansoff matrix proved the strategies used to grow their business and adapt it through the **change** by acquiring technology, merchants, and customers which was then financially proven to lead Uber to profitability in the ratio analysis using the GPM, NPM, and ROCE ratios. However, the investigation conducted was limited as this acquisition only occurred 3 years ago when writing this paper. Secondly, the internal websites and research conducted which originated from Uber was likely to be biased and hence could skew my findings. For future investigations into Uber's acquisition of Postmates, it is important to look at the financials and growth strategies over a long period of time. Furthermore, by looking further into Postmates' financials and their growth strategies, there will be a clearer understanding of their contribution to Uber's profitability and their own independent business respectively. Additionally, more

research into the market and the companies competing with uber will provide a more holistic perspective. Overall, Uber's acquisition of Postmates was successful and has led them to become more profitable.

BIBLIOGRAPHY + APPENDICES OMITTED

3. EXAMPLE THREE (24/25)

Research Question: How does Twitter's transformation, rebranding, and overall change into "X Corp" impacted its business' profitability?

Key concept: Change

Author: K.V

Session: May 2024

Level: SL

<u>Marks Received: 24/25</u>

Key Concept: Change

Internal Assessment in IBDP Business Management

How does Twitter's transformation, rebranding, and overall change into "X Corp" impacted its business' profitability?

Word count: *1800*

Session: *May 2024*

Personal Code: *lbw456*

Contents

1. Introduction

In April 2023, Twitter - a highly influential social media platform - was revealed to undergo a major rebranding, changing its corporate name into "X Corps"[1]. Leading to the rebranding, Twitter was acquired by billionaire and CEO of a bazillion companies, Elon Musk, in October 2022, and has since undergone major **changes** including restructuring, downsizing, and the eventual rebranding[2]. This **change** reflects Elon's commitment to diversifying Twitter's business, from a social media platform into "an everything app" that would undertake multiple common functions altogether - social networking, shopping, ride booking, payment, and more[3]. Eight months after the rebranding, Twitter has added a few features with many more being promised. However, multiple other insignificant revenue sources were also introduced and abolished.

Twitter's **change** would result in pre-existing revenue sources getting altered while new ones simultaneously adopted. This leads stakeholders to raise concern about potential impact on the company's profitability; hence, leading to this analysis' research question, "How will Twitter's transformation and rebranding into 'X Corp' impact its profitability?".

2. Methodology

To assess the financial impact of Twitter's **change**, the following business tools are used:

1. The Ansoff Matrix identifies Twitter's product strategy, ergo their revenue sources, associated with the **change**, allowing for evaluation of existing sources and new sources' potential to impact profitability.

2. Profitability Ratios, particularly Net Profit Margin, prior and succeeding the **change** provides concrete analysis of the company's financial trend; hence, the profitability impact of its **change**.

Theses tools are used in conjunction with the following supporting document including financial statistics, interviews, and articles from diverse publications:

---

[1] Supporting Document #1

[2] Supporting Document #1

[3] Supporting Document #1

#	Title	Author	Publication Date
1	"Musk destroyed all that": Twitter's business is flailing after a year of Elon	Dan Milmo	October 27, 2023
2	How Did Twitter Make Money Before Elon Musk Torched It?	Prakash	December 5, 2022
3	How Elon Musk's Twitter Faces Mountain of Debt, Falling Revenue and Surging Costs	Mark Maurer	November 21, 2022
4	Twitter Revenue and Usage Statistics	Mansoor Iqbal	August 10, 2023
5	Linda Yaccarino defends Elon Musk, X, and herself at Code 2023 [FULL INTERVIEW]	Julia Boorstin	September 29, 2023

Table 1: Overview of the supporting documents used for this analysis

As these documents include factual statistics, company statements, and external research, they would present the topic in a complete, comprehensive, and unbiased manner.

3. Analysis of Findings

3.1 Ansoff Matrix

The Ansoff Matrix is a business tool that strategize growth strategies by identifying different products/service and evaluating their risks[4]. Hence, it would allow for analysis of the risks and effectiveness of both Twitter's pre-existing sources and new ones associated with the **change**.

---

[4] Peterdy K. Ansoff matrix. Corporate Finance Institute. Published 2023. https://corporatefinanceinstitute.com/resources/management/ansoff-matrix/

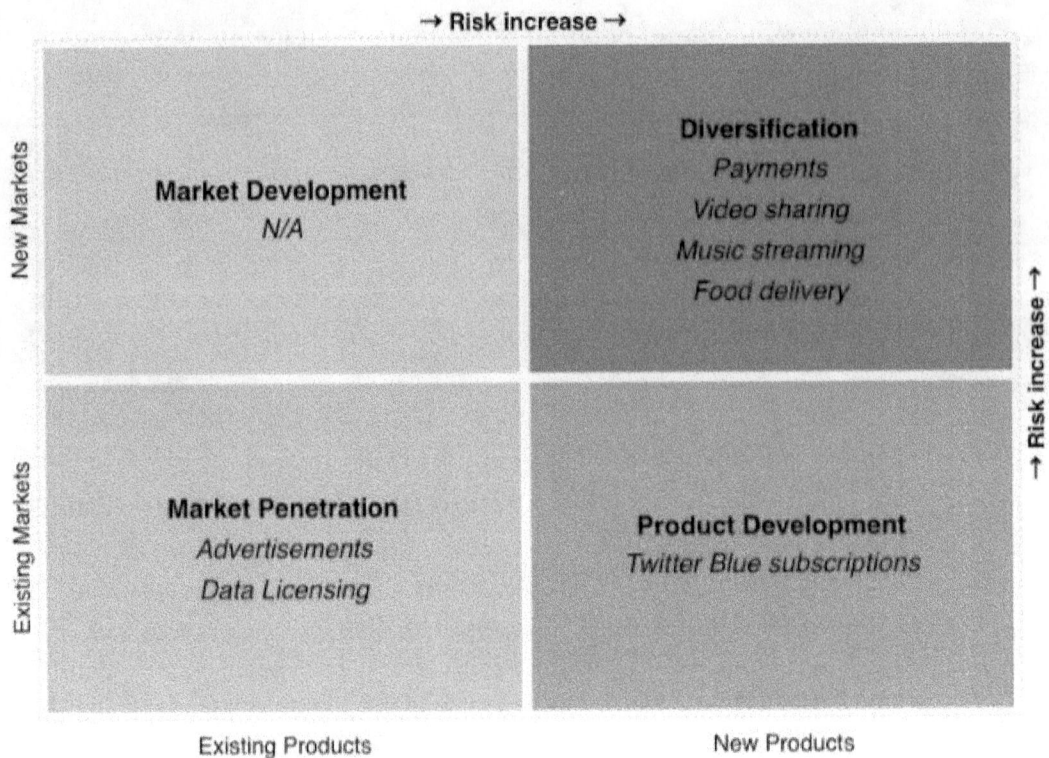

Figure 1: Ansoff Matrix for Twitter classifying its old and new sources of revenue

1. *Market Penetration* - this sector consist of the company's existing offers in a market where the firm already operates; hence, it involves the lowest risk. Advertisements and data licensing, which has historically been Twitter's main and sole revenue sources, fall under this category during the company's **change**[5].

Advertisements: is the primary source of Twitter's revenue[6]. In 2021, advertisements accounted for 89% of total revenue, and was on a growth path of 41% between 2020 and 2021[7]. Furthermore, as Twitter consistently ranked "a solid 3rd or 4th option" among digital advertisers — which is a remarkable accomplishment accounting for Twitter's low number of users versus competitors[8] —, it would be advantageous to further utilize this revenue source as it is highly profitable while carrying the lowest risk.

---

[5] Supporting Document #2

[6] Supporting Document #2

[7] Supporting Document #2

[8] Supporting Document #1

However, since Elon's takeover, Twitter's advertisement revenue has fallen by a stated 50%[9], and Twitter's previously 3rd or 4th advertiser ranking has plummeted to "the bottom of the list"[10]. This is likely triggered by fear of moderation practices and Elon's "capricious" leadership; as such, Elon originally proclaimed on reducing Twitter's reliance on advertising overall by focusing on subscription-based service as an alternative revenue source[11]. Such decision would fail to employ Twitter's reputation in advertising, and now leaves the company at a disadvantage as it eventually ended up attempting to regain advertisers[12].

Data Licensing: composes of the remaining 11% of Twitter's revenue stream in which Twitter sells their user statistics and trends to 3rd-party[13]. Twitter's data licensing revenue was on a slow but stable upward trajectory of 12.3% between 2022 & 2021[14], and there is little controversy surrounding it throughout the company's **change**. However, the company has demonstrated no intention to implement any improvements to it. Such a decision would fail to take advantage of Twitter's only other low-risk and significant revenue source.

2. *Product development:* this sector involves introducing new products or relaunching products into an existing market; hence, it is an average risk strategy. Since the transformation, Twitter Blue has been majorly revamped and relaunched; hence, putting it under product development.

Twitter Blue: is a subscription service that offers extended features to enhance user experience on the platform, like: editing tweets, comment prioritization, and fewer advertisements[15]. However, has been revamped and relaunch under Elon Musk's management intending to become a substantial revenue source. Notably, the monthly subscription fee has been raised to $7.99, a 60% increase, and the infamous "blue tick" is

[9] Supporting Document #3

[10] Supporting Document #1

[11] Supporting Document #3

[12] Supporting Document #5

[13] Supporting Document #2

[14] Supporting Document #2

[15] Beykpour S, Gupta S. Introducing Twitter Blue - Twitter's first-ever subscription offering. blog.twitter.com. Published June 3, 2021. https://blog.twitter.com/en_us/topics/company/2021/introducing-twitter-blue

now given to subscribers instead of genuine account from celebrity and organizations previously[16]. Although product development strategy, such as Twitter Blue, would require careful market & development (R&D), the service has seen rampant **changes**[10] that suggest proper evaluation hasn't been effectively done.

From a stakeholder's perspective, such execution of this strategy is highly risky and disadvantageous. Since its relaunch, the service has undergone rampant **changes**, faced issues of impersonation due to the paid check mark[17], and Twitter CEO Linda Yaccarino appeared uninformed of Elon's intention to substantialize the service[18]. Although Twitter Blue statistics has been improving following the relaunch, it still faces a low subscription of 600,000 users generating $5 million a month[19]. This figure is insufficient to cover for Twitter's loss in advertisement revenue, and is insignificant compared to competitors such as the $20 million monthly average revenue of Snapchat+[20]. However, Snapchat+'s $20 million is still a relatively low figure when compared to its revenue sources such as advertisements. Therefore, this suggest that subscription services are not a large enough revenue source, and even if Twitter Blue gain a much higher degree of success, it would not yield satisfactory return.

3. *Diversification: this sector involves introducing both new products into a new market; hence, it is the riskiest approach as it accumulates both R&D and market research. This category is where Elon Musk's long-term vision for Twitter, as an "everything app", fall under, and will see Twitter in unknown markets with highly established competitors*

Payments: Even though the mobile payment market is expected to continue growth, it is already saturated with highly established companies; however, preferences still vary substantially between countries[21]. This suggest a still changing market which reduces

---

[16] Supporting Document #1

[17] Supporting Document #1

[18] Supporting Document #5

[19] Supporting Document #1

[20] Perez S. Snapchat+ keeps growing as net revenue tops $20M for first time. TechCrunch. Published December 8, 2023. https://techcrunch.com/2023/12/08/snapchat-keeps-growing-as-net-revenue-tops-20m-for-first-time/

[21] Curry D. Mobile Payments App Revenue and Usage Statistics (2021). Business of Apps. Published November 17, 2021. https://www.businessofapps.com/data/mobile-payments-app-market/

Twitter's disadvantage of entering a new market to a certain extent. The company could likely start in the US where the majority of its profitable users is located[22]; however, this would put them in the dominant market of Apple Pay. Apple's reputation and market share is huge, and its seamless incorporation with the highly popular iOS devices makes it very difficult for Twitter to compete. Although Elon's vision to incorporate cryptocurrency could be advantageous as it entices a customer group untouched by other firms[23], it is more likely for Twitter to co-exist with Apple at a smaller scale, but expansion within the US or globally is unlikely. This is because "payment platform is associated with a certain degree of trust that is built over time, making it difficult to make people switch brands"[24].

Others: Very similar obstacles would also exist for the other services Twitter intend to offer. Furthermore, according to CB insights, a company that analyzes tech industry trends, the everything app model has only been successful in Asian markets not European & US markets where the majority of Twitter's user-base is located[25]. Specifically, users of these regions also have a more skeptical view on such an app due to the extensive data that they will share on a singular platform. Hence, government and registration on data privacy will also be much tighter.

Therefore, the Ansoff Matrix showcased the profitability impacts of Twitter's **change** by providing a comprehensive evaluation its old and new revenue sources. Twitter not only deviates from its safest and most significant revenue source, but also intend to embrace the riskier growth strategies that would likely only generate moderate revenue. Therefore, the Ansoff Matrix suggest that the transformation and rebranding is unprofitable, and will result in heavy capital lost in the short-term and only moderate revenue in the long-term if the company prevails the high risks.

Such a comprehensive view is a great strength of the Ansoff Matrix as it presents the individual effects of each growth strategy which significantly informs decision making. However, the Ansoff Matrix only provide theoretical and fact-based prediction, and does not account for non-revenue

---

[22] Supporting Document #4

[23] Bellusci M. Musk Sees Logic for Twitter as a Crypto Payments Platform. www.coindesk.com. Published June 16, 2022. Accessed February 12, 2024. https://www.coindesk.com/business/2022/06/16/musk-sees-logic-for-twitter-as-a-crypto-payments-platform/

[24] Khogeer K. Everything to know about Elon Musk's "everything app." NBC News. Published July 25, 2023. https://www.nbcnews.com/tech/social-media/elon-musk-x-twitter-everything-app-rcna96068

[25] Supporting Document #4

generating **changes** Elon implemented, such as debt or cost savings. Hence, it is necessary to also consider Profit Margin to analyze Twitter's financial trends as well.

3.2 Net Profit Margin

Profitability ratios is used to evaluate a company's profit in relations other features. Specifically, the Net Profit Margin (NPM) compares net profit against sales revenue. Hence, comparing NPM prior and succeeding the **change** provides concrete data of the company's profitability, accounting for all other factors and not just the ability to generate revenue[26]. The ratio is calculated as follows:

$$\text{Net profit margin} = \frac{\text{Net profit}}{\text{Sales revenue}} \cdot 100$$

However, it is important to note that official financial figures after the **change** are unavailable as Elon took the company private by Q3 of 2022[27]. This is a major limitation as data for 2022 could only be estimated using known costs and expenses figures. Regardless, data of Twitter for fiscal years 2020 and 2021 are gathered from supporting document #4 of 2023 and presented[28]:

Year ($mm)	2020	2021
Annual Revenue	3,700	5,000
Net Profit	(1,136)	(221)

Table 1: Twitter annual revenue & PBIT between 2 years prior to transformation

Net profit is estimated by taking data from 2021 and accounting for large **changes** in Twitter's costs and expenses, specifically, its costs of revenue and interest expenses. Upon entry, Elon Musk immediately started reducing staff by half[29]. This layoff of roughly 3,700 people is estimated to save the company $860 million a year based on the company's most recently disclosed median pay figure[30]. Furthermore, Elon also acquired a loan of $13 billion, in which Twitter now has to pay roughly $1.2 billion a year[31]. Hence, Twitter's net profit in 2021 is taken at ($221) million[32], $860 million is added, and $1.2 billion is subtracted to provide an estimate of the company's net profit:

---

[26] Murphy C. What is net profit margin? Formula for calculation and examples. Investopedia. Published March 6, 2022. https://www.investopedia.com/terms/n/net_margin.asp

[27] Supporting Document #4

[28] Supporting Document #4

[29] Supporting Document #3

[30] Supporting Document #3

[31] Supporting Document #3

[32] Supporting Document #4

$$Estimated\ Net\ Profit\ 2022 = (221) + 860 + (1200) \approx (561)$$

Hence, using the complete data table throughout the transformation:

Year ($mm)	Before change 2021	After change 2022
Annual Revenue	5,000	3,300
Net Profit	-221	-561

Table 2: Twitter annual revenue & net profit throughout its transformation with 2022 net profit being estimated

The profit margin for each year is obtained:

Year ($mm)	Before change 2021	After change 2022
Calculations	$\frac{-221}{5000} \cdot 100$	$\frac{-561}{3300} \cdot 100$
Profit Margin	(4.42%)	(17%)

Table 3: Calculations for Twitter's profit margin throughout the change

These number shows the percentage of sales revenue that translates into profit once direct costs have been subtracted; hence it is a great measure of profitability. The negative values indicate Twitter was already making a loss several years before Elon's acquisition. This was likely due to the turbulent situation of these years, including Black Lives Matter protests and Covid-19 pandemic causing advertisers to halt spending.

After Elon's acquisition, Twitter's profit margin dropped significantly. This should be concerning for shareholders as it largely confirms the companies new revenue sources' inability to cover for expenses as predicted by the Ansoff Matrix. If this tendency remains unchanged, which appears to be two years succeeding the **change**, Twitter will encounter devastating liability troubles in the upcoming years.

As the profitability ratios have significantly decreased after corporate transformation and rebranding, NPM confirms the Ansoff Matrix's prediction that profitability of Twitter's **change** is not profitable until now and will likely further decline in the long-term when Twitter adopts very high risks for a moderate reward.

4. Conclusions

In conclusion, the Ansoff Matrix not only proved that Twitter' **change** to take advantage of its most crucial and least risky market penetration strategy, its short-term attempt at product development is disorganized and unlikely to yield satisfactory outcome even if successful. Furthermore, the **change** leaves the company relying on the on the riskiest strategy of diversification in the long-term, and will likely generate only moderate revenue.

In addition, the profit margins analysis for the years of 2021 and 2022 showed a further decline of the company's already negative profit margin. This indicates Twitter's drastic cost saving **changes** are not enough to counteract its revenue drop and increased debt payments; hence, the company could encounter liability troubles in the upcoming years.

Hence, the research question, **"How does Twitter's transformation and rebranding into 'X Corp' impacted its business profitability?"**, has been thoroughly analyzed, and based on the findings, it can be concluded that Elon Musk's acquisition, rebranding, and overall **changes** at Twitter will generate losses for the company, instead of profits. Analysis of external supporting documents often emerges a negative themes towards Twitter's **changes**, while statements from the company (through interviews with Linda Yaccarino as CEO in Supporting Document #5) showed ambiguity and unsupported claims. This somewhat implies the haphazard nature of both current internal and external data, and would suggest incorporation of primary research into the analysis given how real financial figures are no longer available when Elon took the company private.

BIBLIOGRAPHY + APPENDICES OMITTED

4. EXAMPLE FOUR (25/25)

Research Question:

To what extent has the Value Creation Process (VCP) allowed Kadokawa's publication

segment to expand?

Key concept: Creativity

Author: Anthew Chong

Session: May 2024

Level: HL

Marks Received: 23/25

BUSINESS MANAGEMENT HL

RESEARCH PROPOSAL

TO: KADOKAWA CORPORATION

RESEARCH QUESTION: To what extent has **the Value Creation Process (VCP)** allowed **Kadokawa's publication segment** to expand? (Creativity)

WORD COUNT: 1798

Table of Contents:

Introduction:

Kadokawa corporation is a media conglomerate and a publicly traded company, with the intention to "revitalise Japanese culture through publishing" in the postwar era. The company was established in 1945 in Tokyo, Japan with a now international company reach, with subsidiaries in the North Americas and in the Asia Pacific region. (Kadokawa) The company has many different business categories that they are successful in, including the Publication business, Video business, Web services business, Game business and IP business. The **unique selling point** of Kadokawa is its unique **creative** content and production style, which they cultivate in Japan and have expanded worldwide. Their main objectives are to create IPs in Japan, expand domestic publishing market share, and create new **creative** hit IPs.

In recent years, Kadokawa has had a significant amount of success in cultivating new **creative** content using the company's **Value Creation Process (VCP)**. Kadokawa hosts many competitions and websites which are used to discover talent. Kadokawa also makes use of apps, such as the Kakuyomu App, which is used to find and search for aspiring authors with new **creative** ideas. This research project "To what extent has the **Value Creation Process (VCP)** allowed Kadokawa's publication segment to expand?" explores the financial, social and marketing aspects of the business to investigate the **creative** cultivation of content through the **VCP** in correlation with the expansion of Kadokawa's publication segment.

Creativity for Kadokawa:

For Kadokawa, **creativity** is a key factor for the company. The investigation will look into the **VCP**, which is the process of discovery and production of new and **creative** ideas, as well as using **creative** ways to discover and nurture talents to create future **creative** productions and novels, such as through competitions, apps, and websites. For the publication sector,

2

Kadokawa relies on generating and identifying creative productions and IPs. For Kadokawa, the VCP is a creative process to develop ideas that can be expanded into IPs. The creative content created through the VCP allows Kadokawa to distinguish its content. Kadokawa's VCP is the embodiment of the creative key concept, as the creative process used to expand.

Methodology employed:

Primary research with existing customers would be conducted in order to realise the impact of the VCP and creative content. The financial accounts and records, SWOT and Ansoff, along with the integrated yearly reports are available to be used to calculate the profitability of content cultivation and Kadokawa's publication segments, along with the spendings on marketing, and the measuring of the company's current position and value.

Table 1: Supporting Documents

Title of supporting document	Source	Web Link
1. Kadokawa Integrated Report 2022	Kadokawa Ltd	https://group.kadokawa.co.jp/media-download/914/075e0a09b9577050/
2. Financial Results for Fiscal Year Ended March 31, 2023	Kadokawa Ltd	https://ssl4.eir-parts.net/doc/9468/ir_material_for_fiscal_ym7/134973/00.pdf
3. FISCO Company research and analysis report into Kadokawa	FISCO	https://web.fisco.jp/platform/report/0946800/6680080020210701002
4. Kadokawa Integrated Report 2023	Kadokawa Ltd	https://group.kadokawa.co.jp/media/ir/media-download/1122/a3baf392a7a76b3b/
5. 出版不況と戦う、角川の未来型メディア戦略 (Kadokawa's futuristic media strategy to combat the publishing	ToyoKeizai Online	https://toyokeizai.net/articles/-/33720

recession)		

Publications and VCP Analysis:

The VCP is based on three key ideas (Source 1,4)

Table 2: VCP key ideas

Creating new intellectual property	Delivering the IPs to new users	Value to clients and individuals
1. Increasing partners such as creators and writers 2. Increasing titles 3. Creating creative popular IPs 4. Hosting contests to find more prospective writers 5. Using the app Kakuyomu (A writing app) to find new writers and titles to produce	1. Internationally; Bookwalker 2. Locally; Niconico 3. Increasing book stores which carry Kadokawa books	1. Hold a wealth of creative content which could make each individual happy in their own way 2. Diverse content to promote mutual understanding

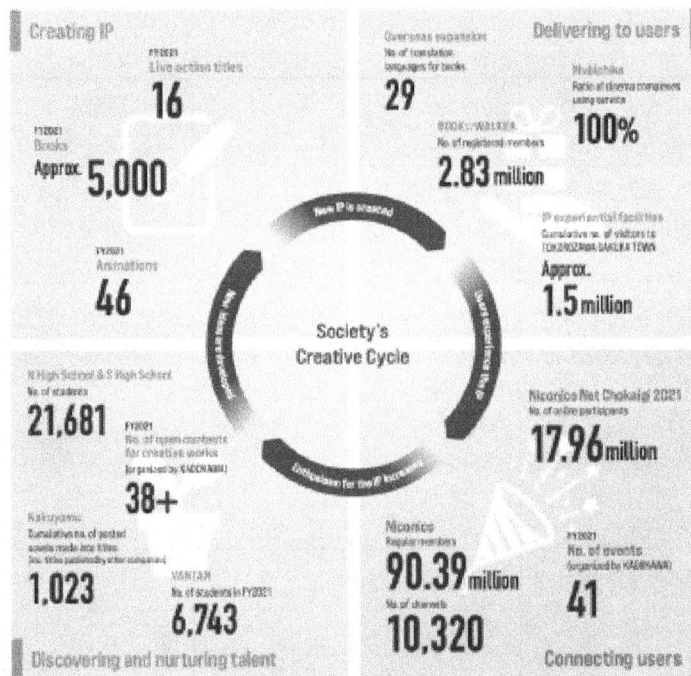

Fig. 1 Kadokawa's Value Creation Process

SWOT Analysis:

Figure 2: SWOT (Xhienne)

SWOT ANALYSIS

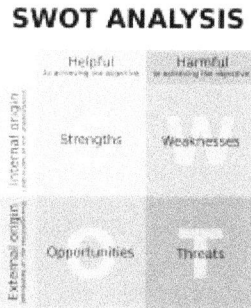

Table 3: SWOT

Strengths	Weaknesses
- Locating and finding talented authors and new publications - Making use of competitions and apps to cultivate creative content - Global expansion of the publishing business through Bookwalker and other web media. - Creative IP deployment, and converting publications into other forms of media and products (Source 4) - Discovering and nurturing talent through Kakuyoku and N and S high school	- Consistently decreasing percentage of company net sales in publication segment - No increase in translation languages, from 2021 to 2023 (Source 1 and Source 4) - Slow but existing profitability increase - Reduced amount of novels publishing from Kakuyoku in 2023 (Source 4) - Limited digital/overseas monetization of content - Mostly traditional production and marketing processes
Opportunities	**Threats**
- Increasing Market Share - Overall rising popularity of Japanese media- including publications in novels, manga and anime. - Expansion of Kadokawa's use of digital media and digital platforms - Expansion of popular novels into manga or animes - Expansion of popular novels, manga and anime into IP products - Expanding fan communities and consumer loyalty - Producing spin-offs such as games and movies - COVID-19, increase in consumption of digital media	- Piracy of content reducing both overseas and local sales - Shueisha and Kodansha's growth in market share - Creators publishing directly online - Business model highly dependent on new creative ideas. - Censorship by major countries would remove the viability of international expansion into regions close to Japan and with a major consumer base. - Shifting demographics may mean a high loss in profits and in market share. - International economic slowdown or inflation would decrease overall spending on entertainment or leisure, thus profits.

6

Through the SWOT analysis, Kadokawa uses the **VCP** in order to bring upon a set of offensive strategies. A strength of Kadokawa meets an opportunity, as the cultivation of strong content through creative factors such as; Kakuyomu and different events allowed Kadokawa to expand largely. It also strengthened the company's position and profitability in the large Japanese market.

Ansoff Matrix:

The Ansoff Matrix will be used to analyse the direction of the company (Sources 1, 3, 4, 5)

Figure 3: Ansoff Matrix (Reiling)

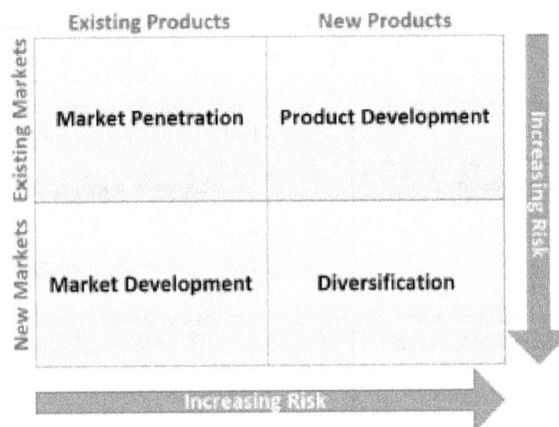

The Ansoff matrix is a tool used to determine the placement of a company in markets and opportunities. It is important to use the Ansoff matrix to analyse Kadokawa as the company's position on its map can show the expansion of Kadokawa's publication segment.

New Markets:

Kadokawa, in 2021, broke into the North American and European market (Source 1, 3, 4) through subsidiaries such as J-novel. They had a large influx of subscribers to Bookwalker, the English manga app released by Kadokawa, with 2.83 million members in 2021 (Source 1). In 2022, Bookwalker had expanded to have 3.5 million members globally, with the app being mainly used by English-speaking members. This is a prime example of expanding into new markets.

New Products

Kadokawa also constantly creates new products and creative intellectual properties through its publishing sector. Kadokawa expanded by translating more of their publications into 29 different languages, breaking into an untapped market. In 2021, Kadokawa used Kakuyomu and other competitions to recruit new writers (Source 1). With this method, Kadokawa cultivated a high amount of creative content from competitions and Kakuyomu. In 2021, 1,023 novels from Kakuyomu were published into novels by Kadokawa (Source 1). The VCP also led the company to host 38 creative works competitions, in which they found creative ideas with a positive outlook. Of the 5,000 novels published in 2021, nearly ⅕ were creative ideas found through Kakuyomu and published into novels. Kadokawa's VCP fits into the Diversification sector of the Ansoff Matrix.

Metrics for Growth

It is extremely important to define growth. In this investigation, the growth of the company will be measured with the following metrics:

Table 4: Growth (Source 1,2,3,4)

	Financial performance of the publication sector	Statistics and publications	Outlook and intellectual property
1	Sales per year	Interest in products	Popularities of the IPs
2	Sales revenue growth year-over-year	Publications per annum	Outlook of the company
3	Profit margins trends	Users on the Kakuyoku App	Strengths, weaknesses, opportunities and threats to Kadokawa
4	Maintaining/growing market share percentage	Success of the Kakuyoku app	The success of bookwalker
5		Size and loyalty of	Niconico video sharing

8

		recurring customer/reader base	platform (IP)
6		Trends in the market	

Ratio and Financial Analysis:

Table 5: Sales Growth Analysis- publication (Source 1,2,4)

	Publication Segment Revenue	Percentage of company net sales in publication segment
Fiscal Year 2018	¥112.7B	60%
Fiscal Year 2019	¥115.96B	61%
Fiscal Year 2020	¥117.3B	59%
Fiscal Year 2021	¥129.58B	58%
Fiscal Year 2022	¥132.97B	56%
Fiscal Year 2023	¥139.99B	53%
CAGR FY 2018-2023 (Compound annual growth rate)	4.5%	-2.04%

CAGR is calculated by inputting the $\left(\left(\frac{Endvalue}{Startvalue}\right)^{(1/number\ of\ years)} - 1\right)$, so for example,

with the publication segment's CAGR, it would be $\left(\left(\frac{139.99B}{112.7B}\right)^{(1/5)} - 1\right) = 0.045 = 4.5\%$

94

Figure 4: Value of the Publishing industry (出版科学研究所 Shuppan Kagaku)

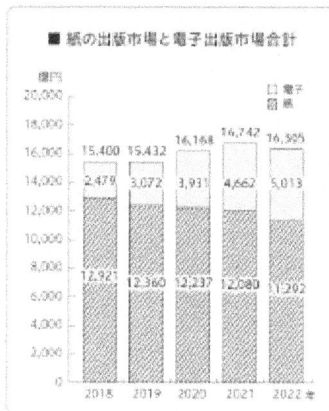

Table 6: Publication margin comparison 2018 to 2022 (Source 2, Kadokawa, Shin Bunka, Shueisha, Shogakukan and Zenrin)

	Shueisha	Kodansha	Kadokawa	Shogakukan	Zenrin
2018	14.3%	10.1%	5.3%	9.2%	15.6%
2019	16.2%	11.3%	6.3%	10.1%	16.8%
2020	13.8%	12.0%	5.3%	10.6%	14.9%
2021	18.5%	13.2%	9.9%	11.8%	16.2%
2022	15.7%	12.5%	13.1%	11.3%	15.4%
CAGR	3.89%	4.71%	10.5%	4.48%	- 0.96%

Profit margin can be calculated with the formula:

$$Profit\ Margin\ =\ Net\ Profit\ /\ Net\ Sales$$

For Kadokawa's 2018 publication sector: (Units in Billion of yen)

$$(Segment\ Profit\ of\ 6,000\ /\ Segment\ Sales\ of\ 112,691)\ =\ 0.053\ =\ 5.3\%$$

I will only be calculating the publication sector's profit margins. For CAGR, the same formula as shown (Table 5) will be used.

Table 7: Market Share Comparison (Source 2, Kadokawa, Shin Bunka, Shueisha, Shogakukan and Zenrin)

	Shueisha	Kodansha	Kadokawa	Shogakukan	Zenrin
2018	14.11%	9.47%	7.32%	7.60%	0.325%
2019	14.38%	9.84%	7.53%	7.79%	0.340%
2020	13.09%	9.74%	7.24%	7.59%	0.337%
2021	13.73%	9.83%	7.76%	7.55%	0.341%
2022	14.46%	10.45%	8.17%	6.48%	0.362%
CAGR	3.6%	4.12%	4.4%	-3.5%	1.1%.

The market share can be calculated with this formula:

$$\frac{Total\ sales\ of\ the\ company}{Total\ sales\ of\ the\ market} \times 100\% = Market\ Share$$

For the sample of Kadokawa in 2022, we can refer back to Graph 1 for the value of the publication market in Japan in 2022, which was ¥1.63 trillion yen. The total sales of the publication sector for that year sat at ¥132,972 million yen, therefore:

$$\frac{¥132,972}{¥1,630,000,000,000} \times 100\% = 8.17\%$$

Therefore, for 2022, the market share for the publication sector of Kadokawa is 8.17%. Kadokawa.

Figure 5: Market Share for the top 5 companies.

Market Share for the top 5 publishing companies in Japan from 18-22

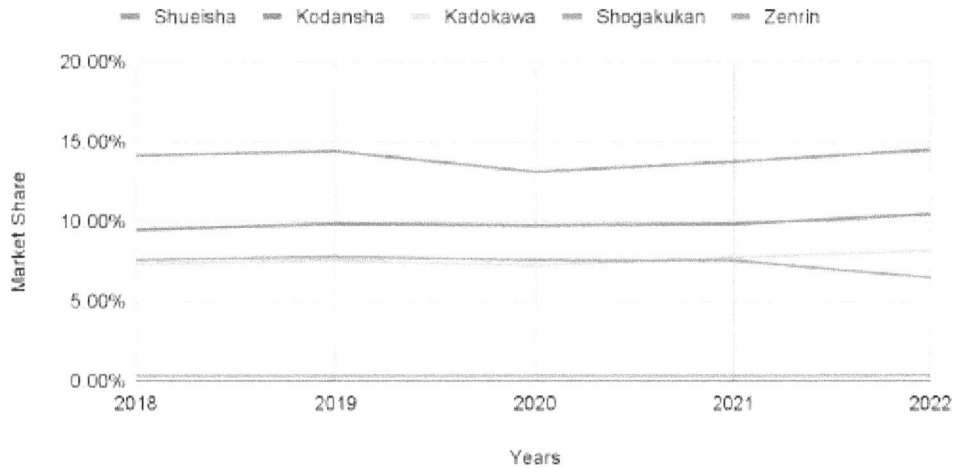

Figure 5 shows that Shogakukan was higher than Kadokawa in market share, but after the

VCP was implemented in 2020, there has been an obvious upwards trend on market share,

with Kadokawa overtaking Shogakukan.

Research and further investigation:

Although the data shown by Kadokawa and FISCO seems positive, not many other sources

give further information into Kadokawa's VCP. The validity of Source 3, the FISCO report

independent of Kadokawa, also gives further insight into Kadokawa's data and information,

along with its validity, since it is not too different to the analysis by FISCO. The overreliance

of this investigation on Kadokawa's own data could be a detriment to the investigation on

data bias. Not many negatives were published on the reports, although the FISCO analysis

(Source 3) showed some downsides of the company. We can see that "The Company is

aiming to increase the number of new creative IPs from approximately 5,000 a year to

around 6,000 a year." (Source 3). The FISCO report shows some level of optimism and

12

insight, but the Kadokawa 2023 integrated report (Source 4) shows that there is no increase in IP creation, with it still sitting at 5,000 per fiscal year. (Lawton)

Primary Research:

Conducting a primary investigation into the topic would give a further unbiased insight into Kadokawa's VCP and if it works. This primary investigation will be conducted on a number of consumers by random sampling near a Japanese manga store in Hong Kong.

Graph 6: Primary Research on satisfaction with Kadokawa's latest publishings

Responses from question "From a scale of 1-10 how would you rate Kadokawa's latest publishings in the 2023 season?"

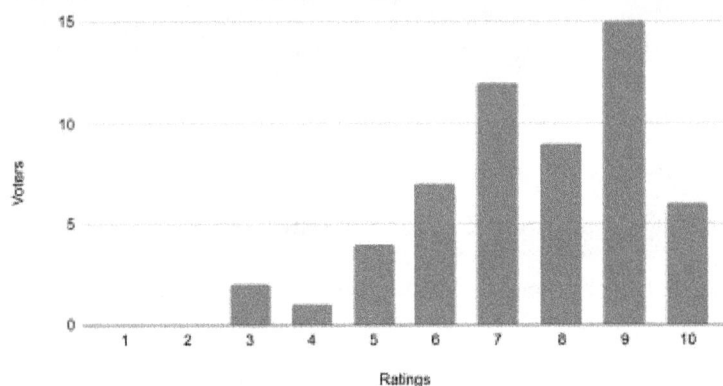

This investigation and primary research shows that Kadokawa's analysis and information is quite accurate, with the mean rating being a 7.27. Asking the same question but for another company; Shueisha, would give further insight into Kadokawa's standings.

Graph 7: Primary Research on satisfaction with Shueisha's latest publishings

Interview into "From a scale of 1-10 how would you rate
Shueisha's latest publishings in the 2023 season?"

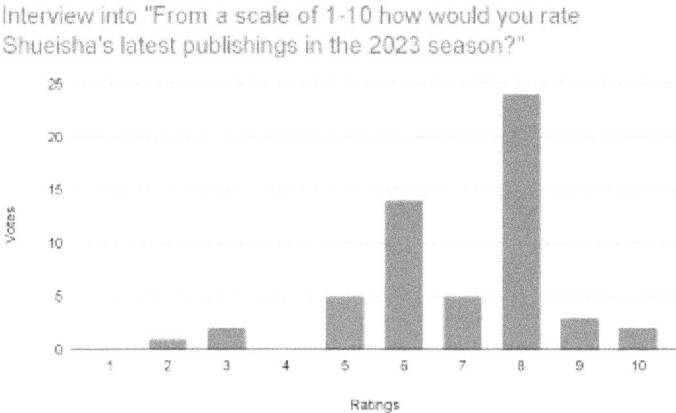

Shueisha got an average rating of 6.98. This portrays Kadokawa's recent creative

productions as more highly rated by this random sample size of people in Hong Kong.

Furthermore, Source 5, the interview with Director Tatsuo Sato, gives further insight into the

company's creative ideals. He said ""From analog to digital" and "from local to global". We

are trying to establish a business portfolio based on creative content" This gives us an insight

into Kadokawa's views on content. This source shows us an insider view into his ideas of

expanding the company using the VCP.

Evaluation:

Through all the analysis, suggestions will now be made in relation to expanding the

company's publication segment, along with examining and concluding on the effect of the

VCP and whether the creative publishings through the process has been successful. As can

be seen in Table 2, the percentage of net sales that can be attributed to the publication

segment has dropped below 50% in 2023. This may mean a decrease in reliance on the

publication segment, but may also mean a decrease in effectiveness of the VCP. As can be

seen in Table 3, the profitability margin has increased with a CAGR of 10.5%, which is much

higher than that of its competitors, but the problem is that it is still too slow for a company

14

looking to expand quickly, which may show a downside. The amount of new **creative** publication IP sourced from Kakuyoku in 2023 is only 374, as compared to the previous 1023 in 2021, this is an obvious decrease. Consequently, Piracy of the content created by Kadokawa could largely reduce profits, since users and consumers are much more likely to look for free or alternate methods to read and watch the content created and cultivated by Kadokawa. (Mandal) Kadokawa could enforce stricter digital security, along with applying further pressure on the companies or websites which offer these pirated contents legally. Although this is true, the increasing market shares of Kadokawa can be seen in Table 4, which proves a positive growth of the company. The business model of Kadokawa would fail if they are unable to source **creative** new ideas through the **VCP**. Competitors have had this problem through their other methods of sourcing content and creating IP, such as with Shogakukan, who is rapidly losing market share.

Conclusion:

In conclusion, the **VCP** has brought great profit to Kadokawa, although there have been some downsides and the growth is not as fast as expected, as shown in Source 1, 3 and 4, and by the profitability ratio. The outlook shown in sources 2 and 5 along with the primary investigation, gives an insight into the future of the company, and gives an analysis into the company. Through the financial analysis, the increase in profit and market share in 2020, when the **VCP** started, we can realise the large impact of the process upon Kadokawa's **creative** productions and publishings.

BIBLIOGRAPHY + APPENDICES OMITTED

5. EXAMPLE FIVE (22/25)

Research Question: Should Disney+ change its current pricing strategy to increase its revenue and subscriber retention in the US?

Key concept: Change

Author: Ken R.F

Session: May 2024

Level: HL

<u>Marks Received: 22/25</u>

Research Question:

Should Disney+ change its current pricing strategy to increase its revenue and subscriber retention in the US?

Key Concept: Change

Personal Code: krf046

Exam Session: May 2024

Word count: 1797 (excluding in-text citations)

TABLE OF CONTENTS

INTRODUCTION

Disney+ is an American streaming service owned by the Walt Disney Company (SD. 1). It first entered the market in 2019 with penetration pricing, where it set initially low prices, helping it reach 100 million subscribers in a year despite the presence of market leaders like Netflix (SD. 5). However, a lot has **changed** recently; the market has become increasingly saturated, making competition fiercer. Disney+ is no longer the only affordable option and is struggling to grow its sales and subscribers (Fitzgerald).

The CEO Bob Iger's original plan was to raise prices incrementally by $1 yearly (SD. 5) owing to penetration pricing. However, with new 2024 subscribers and profitability goals in sight (Ace), there is a need for strategy **change**. In the US, they have been raising their prices in hopes of accelerating their earnings. The most recent plan for another price **change** was announced at the end of 2023: the company will raise its ad-free service by $3 (SD. 4). If they undertake this plan, Disney+ will be shifting to value-based pricing, as they are planning to justify their high prices with their high-quality content (Ace). This raises the question: *Should Disney+ change its current pricing strategy to increase its revenue and subscriber retention in the US?*

Connecting to the concept of **change**, I will explore whether the company should adapt to the evolving streaming industry by modifying its pricing strategy from penetration to value-based. I will use a revenue-subscriber analysis to observe how past price **changes** have affected the company, force field analysis to weigh the potential impact of a future price **change**, and a position map to determine if they are in the position to raise their prices in this newly **changed** market.

FINDINGS AND ANALYSIS

I.   Statistical Analysis

I will calculate the percentage **changes** in Disney+'s historical data and analyze them against past price hikes. This will give an insight into how customers normally react to price **changes**, allowing me to evaluate if raising their price and committing to value-based pricing will boost the company's revenue growth and subscriber retention.

This will be supported by SD. 1. It is important to consider that the website acquires the data from the company's annual financial reports, meaning that any selective disclosure or financial manipulation by the company will be reflected on this source. Additionally, due to the lack of availability of region-specific data in the public domain, I can only rely on this global data, which is not completely reflective of the US market.

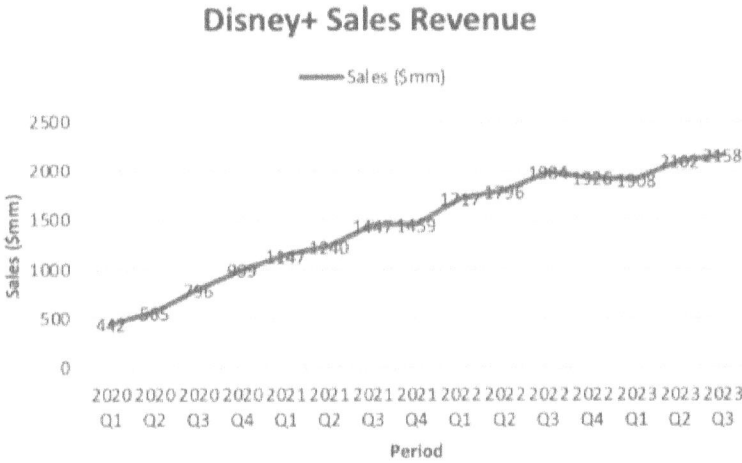

Fig. 1. Sales Revenue of Disney+ in 2020 - 2023 (SD. 1)

Table 1

Percentage Difference of Disney+'s revenue in 2020 - 2023

Fiscal Year	Percentage Difference/Fiscal Year
2020	$\frac{(999-442)}{442} \times 100 =$ **126.0%**
2021	$\frac{(1459-1147)}{1147} \times 100 =$ **27.2%**
2022	$\frac{(1926-1717)}{1717} \times 100 =$ **12.2%**
2023	$\frac{(2158-1908)}{1908} \times 100 =$ **13.1% (only 3 quarters)**

Calculation based on data adapted from SD. 1.

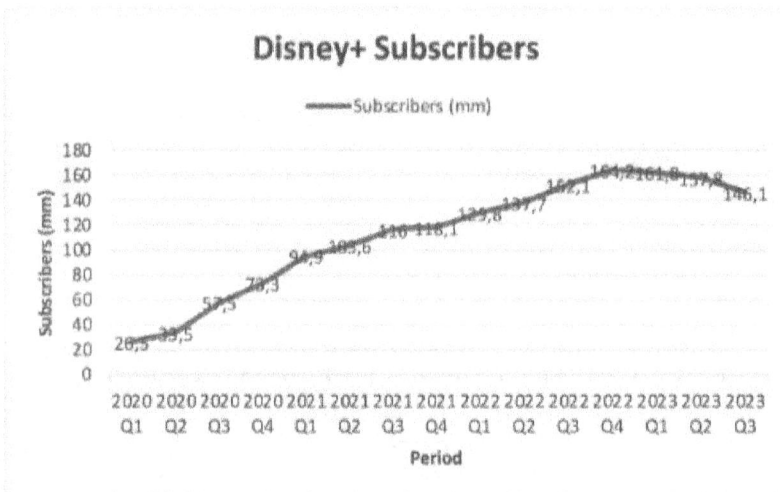

Fig. 2. Subscribers of Disney+ in 2020 - 2023 (SD. 1)

Table 2

Percentage Difference of Disney+'s subscribers in 2020 - 2023

Fiscal Year	Percentage Difference/Fiscal Year
2020	$\frac{(73.3-26.5)}{26.5} \times 100 =$ **176.6%**
2021	$\frac{(118.1-94.9)}{94.9} \times 100 =$ **24.4%**
2022	$\frac{(164.2-129.8)}{129.8} \times 100 =$ **26.5%**
2023	$\frac{(164.2-129.8)}{129.8} \times 100 =$ **-9.7% (only 3 quarters)**

Calculation based on data adapted from SD. 1.

With penetration pricing, Disney+ enjoys substantial growth in subscribers and revenue, where both growth rates exceeded 100% in the first fiscal year. After a $1 price hike in Q1 of 2021 from $6.99 to $7.99 (SD. 5), the revenue growth drastically dropped to only 27.2% (see Table 1) and 24.4% for subscribers (see Table 2). This suggests that Disney+'s services are price demand elastic, whereby a minor price increase results in a significant **change** in the quantity demanded.

In Q4 of 2022, Disney+ raised their prices again by $3, but this time, only for their ad-free services (SD. 5). This **change** saw a considerable decrease in subscribers in 2023, with a churn rate of -9.7% (see table 2). Contrastingly, however, the revenue increased from 12.2% in 2022 to 13.1% in 2023 (see table 1). This discrepancy between the revenue and subscriber counts implies that these two factors do not necessarily align. Although the price hike may have deterred some consumers, there are enough users who decide to purchase the more expensive ad-free plan, resulting in rising revenues. This implies that while Disney+'s service is price elastic to some consumers who only subscribed due to its initial low price, there are also less price-sensitive consumers who subscribe to Disney+ for its content, hence their willingness to pay higher.

It can be deduced that if Disney+ continues to raise its prices, it may deter some price-sensitive consumers and worsen subscriber retention. However, at the same time, it may also boost Disney+'s revenue and help it achieve its profitability goal, as there are also customers who believe that the high prices are worth it for Disney+'s service. This supports the decision to **change** to a value-based pricing model as long as the quality of their content remains **unchanged**, but only in boosting revenue.

II.   Force Field Analysis

This will examine the driving and restraining forces for **changing** Disney+'s pricing strategy to value-based pricing. Each force is rated from 1 to 5 in terms of its probable impact on boosting revenue and retaining subscribers.

This will be primarily supported by SD. 2, a survey by an official market research company, "OnePoll," making it credible. However, it only surveyed 1,000 Americans, which means it may be inadequate to represent millions of consumers. SD. 3 will also aid this; a CBS News interview with an expert who can provide an unbiased review regarding the potential impact of the planned price **change**. However, due to the interview being with just one person, his reports may have limited perspective. Using both sources will thus form a more holistic analysis, with a specific focus on external stakeholders' perspectives.

Driving Force		Restraining Force	
Disney+ maintains exclusive content. By targeting children and specific fan bases like Marvel and Star Wars, Disney+ operates in a segmented market (SD. 1). This allows them to gain a stronger position in each segment, where users are less deterred from	5	The streaming industry is experiencing price inflation (SD. 3). If Disney+ increases its price along with its competitors, it will lose its competitive advantage. The CEO initially wanted to make Disney+ the cheapest streaming service to appear as the best value proposition (SD. 5), but the	4

	raising prices, thus maintaining subscriber retention.		price hike will eliminate this differentiation, making sales harder.	
4	Over half of users do not keep close track of their subscription spending and forget to cancel their free trials (SD. 2). This indicates audiences' lack of attentiveness towards prices, implying that a price **change** may continue to retain subscribers.	Adopting value-based pricing, which will come with an increase in price.	28% of Disney+ users claim they would cancel subscriptions if higher prices were enforced (SD. 2). Thus, the price hike can potentially lead to a ¼ subscriber churn.	5
4	Over half of users subscribe to Disney+ for a specific show (SD. 2). If prices increase, consumers may still be willing to stick around for those.		Actors and writers are on strike, causing a delay in content production (SD. 3). If consumers feel like they are not receiving the promised content to justify increased prices, the company may face high subscriber churn.	1
3	Walt Disney Company has invested billions of dollars to improve Disney+'s library (SD. 3). This can give value to the raised prices, preventing subscriber churn and potentially even attracting new consumers to boost revenue.		The market is becoming more saturated, increasing alternatives. If Disney+ raises its price, it may encourage "service-hopping," where consumers rapidly **change** their subscriptions between different platforms.	4
5	Increasing prices in ad-free plans maximizes revenue sources (SD. 3). Users who do not like ads will pay the higher price, leading to more revenue. At the same time, price-sensitive users will pay the cheaper ad-supported option, which still generates advertising revenue.		If Disney+ raises its price, users will be more motivated to find ways to reduce their spending, such as by sharing accounts with friends and family (SD. 3), thus reducing subscribers.	2

The highest scores (4-5) are assigned to factors that address users' price sensitivity, as they have the greatest influence on revenue and/or subscriber retention. Lower scores (1-3) are assigned to factors that have a less substantial impact, such as the workers' strike, which is only temporary, or factors that are already happening regardless of a pricing strategy **change**, such as the common practice of sharing accounts.

The driving force sums up to 21 points, and the restraining force to 16 points. Many of the driving forces suggest that some subscribers will not **change** their habits and continue subscribing even if prices increase due to their perceived quality and exclusivity of Disney+'s content. This indicates high price insensitivity, aligning with the deductions made from the statistical analysis. It confirms that **changing** to value-based pricing may be in the best interest of the company's revenue and subscribers.

III. Position Map

The recent **change** in the industry following the large influx of brands calls for the need for a position map, which assesses whether the company is in a position to raise its prices based on consumers' current perceived value of the brand compared to its competitors. The price positioning will be based on personal checking of each company's prices, and the quality positioning will be supported by SD. 4. As a survey conducted on 1,000 avid US streamers, this source reflects accurate perceptions of the target market. However, it is important to acknowledge that the sample size may not be sufficient to represent the entire market.

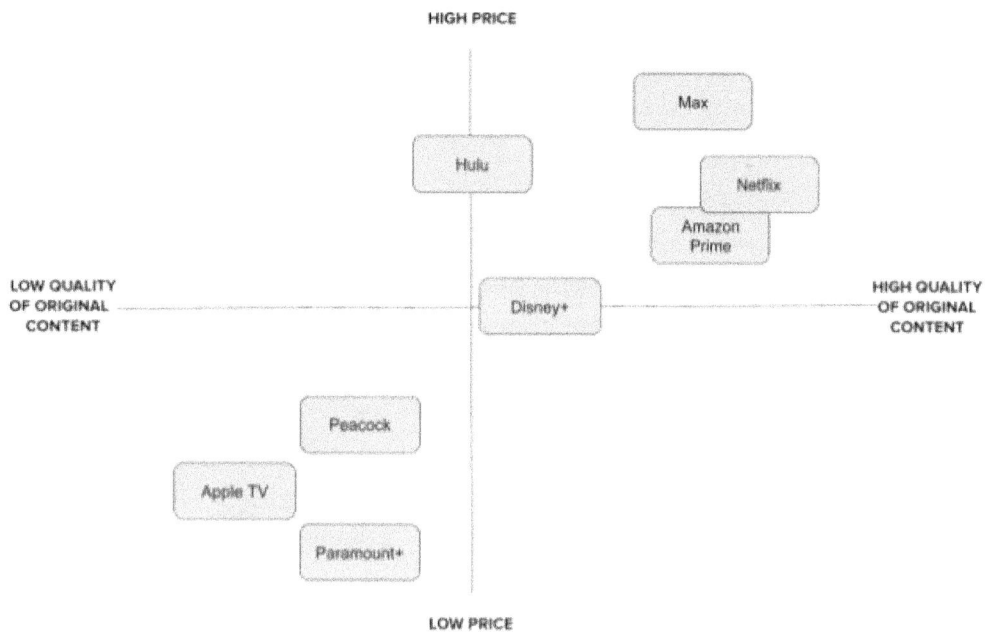

Fig. 3. Position Map for the Streaming Industry in the US; Price Against Quality (SD. 4)

Although the previous analysis suggested that Disney+ can **change** to value-based pricing by raising its price due to its high quality and exclusive content, this tool shows that, in comparison to its competitors, Disney+'s content is actually still relatively average. Turns out, consumers believe three other companies offer better content. However, these three companies are also more expensive than Disney+, indicating that Disney+ still has a competitive advantage as long as they keep prices low.

This position map also presents that Disney+ is still in the middle price range. This means they are still in a feasible position to raise its price, but only incrementally. The planned $3 may be too much, potentially causing price-sensitive users to switch to significantly cheaper options—like Peacock, Apple TV, and Paramount—and consumers who prioritize high-quality content to **change** to the alternatives with similar prices yet better value proposition: Netflix, Amazon Prime, and Max. Therefore, this indicates that entirely **changing** to a value-based pricing model must be reconsidered.

CONCLUSION

Based on the findings above, Disney+ should consider raising its price and **changing** to a value-based pricing model to increase its revenue and subscriber retention in the United States.

The statistical analysis reveals that previous price increases have resulted in rising revenue, attributed to existing customers willingly paying more due to the perceived value of the content. Thus, by **changing** to value-based pricing, Disney+ can leverage the loyalty of its price-insensitive consumers to reap financial benefits. The force field analysis supports this, showcasing driving forces that indicate a significant segment of US consumers who are unlikely to **change** their habits if prices increase, which suggests that a price hike will continue to retain their customers. On the other hand, the position maps signify that many consumers perceive Disney+'s quality as relatively average compared to some competitors. Therefore, if Disney+ still proceeds to adopt this strategy **change**, the company must approach this with caution, as a sudden and significant price hike may pose a risk of customers opting for alternatives with better value propositions. A price hike must be implemented simultaneously with an investment in their content to ensure that the quality matches the added value customers are paying.

It must be considered that my arguments remain applicable under the assumption that market conditions remain relatively stable over the period of the planned price **change**; a significant market shift may affect the success of this proposed strategy. Therefore, to make better judgments, a further extension to this investigation is to assess external market conditions.

BIBLIOGRAPHY + APPENDICES OMITTED

6. EXAMPLE SIX (21/25)

Research Question:

What is the extent to which Apple's decision to exclude chargers from its product packaging contributes to the advancements of **sustainability** objectives and increases profitability?

Key concept: Sustainability

Author: Omar

Session: May 2024

Level: SL

Marks Received: 20/25

<u>IB DP Business Management Research Project</u>

Research question:

''what is the extent to which Apple's decision to exclude chargers from its product packaging contributes to the advancements of sustainability objectives and increases profitability?''

Key Concept: Sustainability

Examination session: May 2024

Word count: 1760

Declaration of Authenticity:
I confirm that this work is all my own and that this is the final version of this written commentary. I have acknowledged the use of of any information collected from primary or secondary sources. All supporting documents are attached in the appendices. These are contemporary in nature and were written within a maximum of a 3 years prior to submission. All parts in the supporting document that relate directly to this commentary have been highlighted. To addition to the sources that have been acknowledged in the bibliography.

<u>Table of contents:</u>

1. Introduction

Apple Multinational plc, Apple has a diversified product offering ranging from consumer electronics such as tablets, smartphones, and personal computers enabling it to have a prominent position in the global smartphone market. As of the year 2022, Apple holds a substantial market share equal to 28.43% worldwide. Apple's brand value is expected at a remarkable $355.08 billion, strengthening as one of the world's most valuable brands in 2022. (BBC News)

In 2020 Apple's strategic decision to eliminate the charger from iPhone 11 packaging has garnered significant attention due to its commitment in terms of environmental **sustainability**. Apple released its new smartphone the iPhone 12, without earbuds and charger. This has resulted in an increased criticism that customers must purchase accessories separately if needed. (BBC News)

Apple aims to eliminate chargers from its iPhone packaging to reduce electronic waste by encouraging the customer to use their existing chargers and, at the same time, reduce the environmental impact of manufacturing and disposing of chargers. The key driving factor behind eliminating the charger is **sustainability** as well as reducing production and packaging expenses. With the launch of the iPhone 12 in 2020, Apple stopped including power adapters and headphones in iPhone boxes. (BBC News)

The objective of this written commentary is to assess the following the Research Project question "To what extent has Apple's decision to exclude chargers from its product packaging contributed to the advancement of **sustainability** objectives and increased profitability?"

2. Methodology

The written report consists of both quantitative and qualitative research methods. A diversified set of five supporting documents sourced from sustainability reports, annual reports, media articles, and online journals. A triple bottom was utilized to explore the goals of sustainability. From a financial aspect, the use of ratio analysis specifically profitability ratio to measure the extent to which Apple's charger removal reduces costs of production and increases overall profitability.

3. Discussion of the findings

Figure (1): Triple bottom line (people, profit and planet) (Debnath)

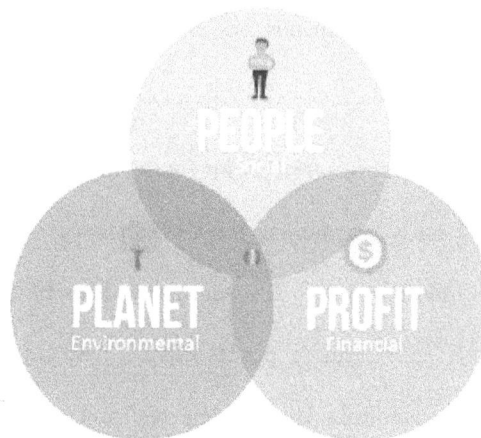

4.1 Triple Bottom line

TBL was first created in 1994 by John Elkington, it was created because he mentioned that ''a company can well be financially successful yet harm the social or ecological environment in which it is embedded." For that reason, he decided to create the TBL. ("What Is the 'Triple Bottom Line'?")

Evaluating Apple's decision to remove chargers through the TBL framework exhibits a balance between environmental considerations, social responsibility, and financial outcomes. Apple can contribute to sustainability objectives by contemplating the planet and people. This universal approach reflects a growing trend in business strategy where sustainability is integrated into decision-making processes. Apple has been participating and investing in many different sustainability initiatives.

- **Economic**

  Apple has saved over six billion dollars by not including chargers and earphones (Cowling) However, despite the reduction in box accessories content, the price of the iPhone has increased compared to the previous model, yet this increase might be attributed to other technological advancements. As mentioned, one of Apple's main vision and mission statement is to put people first.

  Profit holds more than ordinary financial profits for a company. It can entail creating more income ethically and fairly, positioning with collaborators and suppliers who share philanthropic values, and succeeding financial agreements to investors, creditors, and employees dependably. Furthermore, profits expand, help, and aid the community by paying taxes rapidly, supporting local businesses, and participating in community development enterprises. This broader understanding of profit encourages companies to prioritize sustainability and to have a better social responsibility.

- **Environmental**

The unused and discarded electronic appliances contribute to electronic waste (Cowling). In 2022, recycling and composting efforts sanctioned Apple to achieve a waste diversion rate of

71 percent — up from 68 percent in 2021 — restricting landfill waste from global operations to about 16,000 metric tons. In 2023, Taiwan Technology Center happen to be the second Apple facility to receive the UL Solutions Zero Waste to Landfill authentication. The data center in Viborg, Denmark, became the third facility to obtain TRUE certification in 2023, enrolling the data centers in Mesa, Arizona, and Prineville, Oregon.70 These facilities accomplished TRUE Platinum, the highest certification level. TRUE recognizes facilities that amuse more than 90 percent of waste for recycling, compost, or reuse. (*Product Environmental Report – Apple*).

Apple by removing the chargers and earphones contributed to the reduction of electronic waste, as the phone charger generates over 51,000 tons of e-waste per year (Explainers). This makes us to reconsider to what extent does it help Apple with sustainability by excluding the iPhone charger from the accessory box. The production of these accessories' consumers' natural resources, thereby not including them with every new iPhone, helps in reducing the mining of materials and negative environmental impact involved with manufacturing (Explainers). Removing the charger allows Apple to make the packaging smaller and lighter. Reduction in packaging materials may and will result in less overall waste.

To elaborate more Apple reduced the package contents for each iPhone sold is smaller, attributed to lower emissions from transport, production, and in the long term its disposal. These efforts minimize carbon footprint and reduce electronic waste aligning with environmental sustainability goals. (*Product Environmental Report - Apple*.). Also, if user reclaimed phone chargers, this will lead to reduction in manufacturing of chargers and less corruption of natural resources (Explainers). To elaborate more users who tend to use their old iPhone chargers rather than buying a new one.

Reassuring and promoting users to reuse their phone chargers can substantially lead a reduction in manufacturing demand and improve the environmental impact associated with the production of these universal accessories. By encouraging a culture of charger renovation, consumers actively participate in the obvious **sustainability** efforts directed at minimizing resource exhaustion and environmental deprivation. The persistent manufacturing of chargers consumes valuable natural resources, effects electronic waste, and adds to the inclusive carbon footprint.

In 2020, Apple attained carbon neutrality for its global corporate operations and revealed Apple 2030: a bold strategy to be carbon neutral across its entire value chain by 2030. Apple's plan centers on an aggressive 75 percent reduction in overall carbon emissions from 2015 levels (Apple, "Apple Unveils Its First Carbon Neutral Products"). Although the goal of Apple is to reduce carbon footprint. Apple has been consistently investing in significant financial resources in **sustainability** industries ''In 2023, Apple announced a commitment of additional funds — up to $200 million — to expand the Restore Fund to be managed by Climate Asset Management, a joint venture between HSBC Asset Management and Pollination'' (Apple, Environmental Progress Report). The company has committed to a range of environmental initiatives, involving renewable energy projects, recycling programs, and the use of recycled materials in product manufacturing. There have not been any exact values on how much they have spent on this ongoing procedure.

- **Social**

Apple has faced legal challenges, such as in Brazil, indicating that the decision of removing the charger from the accessory box has ramifications in terms of customer satisfaction. (BBC News) Some customers appreciated this environmental initiative. Yet, some customers are displeased because they must potentially purchase the accessories separately which led to an additional cost and cost cutting measure at the expense.

Settling sustainability goals with broad accessibility is an ongoing challenge. Apple must direct this balance to ensure that the benefits of sustainability are not compromised by segregation certain demographics. Supervising and adjusting strategies based on consumer feedback are critical to addressing these potential limitations.

TBL is a framework that helps decision takers to take the decisions according to the evaluations and discussions made within (Social, Environmental and Economic). These have been discussed and fully explained regarding both the positive and negative impacts on Apple decision on excluding the charger. People and the community in general have been talking and discussing the effect on many different aspects but mainly environmental impacts and how it is a main part within sustainability.

4.3 Financial analysis

Return On Capital Employed of 56.3% ranks in the 95.4% percentile for the sector.

In an aim to conduct a financial analysis to understand the implication of Apple removing charger's ratio analysis specifically Profitability ratios were utilized. Profitability ratios are financial metrics used to assess Apple's ability to generate profit from its operations and investments.

In terms of sales revenue, sales revenue increased by 33.3% between the years 2020-2021 $274,515,000 to $365,817,000, and increased by 7.8% between the years 2021-2022, this suggests an extended increase in demand. However, to look at the profitability ratio would be better. To conclude, a good percentage of ROCE implies that a business is efficiently operating its capital to produce more profits, which is generally observed as an optimistic sign for shareholders and stakeholders.

The GPM increased to 41.76% in 2021 from 38.24% in 2020 and further increased to 43.29% in 2022, this indicates continued improvement in cost management. It's better to glance at the net profit margin as it gives a more precise indication of profitability status as it deducts both direct and indirect costs. The NPM increased from 24.10% to 29.77% between the years 2020-2021, and in 2022 its NPM slightly improved to 30.2%, this suggests that Apple is managing its expenses (production costs).

It is highly essential for Apple to understand the financial implications of Apple's sustainability-focused decision in terms of excluding chargers from product packaging and the impact on its overall financial performance. Profit is Apple's goal, yet Apple's sustainability strategic decision to eliminate chargers from product packaging, the provided analysis does not directly address this as the need for more information on the cost savings achieved by this decision. Apple's decision to exclude chargers and EarPods from iPhone packaging has led to substantial cost savings of $6.5 billion, which means that Apple was able to reduce production and packaging costs simultaneously, contributing positively to profitability. The use of ratio analysis tools may not accurately predict future performance and the current financial health.

Table (1): Financial information from Apple's annual report consisting of sales revenue, gross profit, profit before interest and tax, and Profitability ratio of Apple. (*Yahoo Is Part of the Yahoo Family of Brands*).

The formulas used to calculate the profitability ratios are:

- Return on capital employed (ROCE) = $\left(\frac{Profit\ before\ intrst\ and\ tax}{Capital\ employed}\right) \times 100$

- Gross Profit Margin (GPM): GPM = $\left(\frac{Gross\ profit}{sales\ revenue}\right) \times 100$

- Net Profit Margin (NPM): NPM = $\left(\frac{Net\ profit}{sales\ revenue}\right) \times 100$

	2020	2021	2022
Sales revenue ($)	274,515,000	365,817,000	394,328,000
Gross profit ($)	104,956,000	152,836,000	170,782,000
GPM (%)	38.24%	41.76%	$\frac{170,782,000}{394,328,000} \times$ $100\% = 43.29\%$
Net profit ($)	66,288,000	108,949,000	119,437,000
NPM(%)	24.10%	29.77%	$=$ $\frac{119,437,000}{394,328,000} 100\% = 30.2\%$
Capital employed	$65,339,000	$63,090,000	$50,672,000
ROCE (%)	29.4%	49.1%	56.3%

Conclusion

The conclusions from the analysis, tools, and theories used above imply that Apple is now trying its best to reduce its Carbon Footprint, which will attract more customers. Which answers my research question "what is the extent to which Apple's decision to exclude chargers from its product packaging contributes to the advancements of sustainability objectives and increases profitability?". Not to mention that excluding these chargers would not only make customers use their old chargers more carefully so that it can last longer since chargers won't come with the new iPhone they buy, but it will teach them a variable lesson. Looking at how these initiatives will increase Apple profits according to the estimations in the financial analysis above. This study does not include all the external factors that are concerning it. Extensions could explore the strategy's overall effectiveness and sustainability.

BIBLIOGRAPHY + APPENDICES OMITTED

7. EXAMPLE SEVEN (24/25)

Research Question:

Should the 'SUR' company introduce a Corporate Social Responsibility (CSR) document?

Key concept: Ethics

Author: Miriam Kanner

Session: May 2024

Level: HL

Marks Received: 24/25

Table of Contents

Introduction

In modern society, individuals are becoming increasingly critical of ethical misconduct, whether it includes undermining human rights, being intolerant to minorities, or promoting unhealthy lifestyles. The need to adopt the ethics of mass cultures among companies that supply services to the public is constantly growing. Due to this increasing consumer pattern, it is difficult for small and conceptual businesses like SUR[1] to immediately fit into the ever-changing ethical standards of managerial behaviour.

SUR is a bar founded in 2020 and situated in a dense residential area. The company belongs to the tertiary sector and operates as an LLC[2]. SUR is famous for its party atmosphere, usually accompanied by loud music and alcoholic drinks.

Drawing its inspiration from the free nature of Berlin bars[3], SUR is often confronted with conflicting ethical paradigms in its interactions with the local, more conservative, external stakeholder groups. In the last few years of the bar's existence, conflicts have mainly arisen with local area residents[4] and SUR's social media followers[5]. Experience proves that bar administration often faces inconveniences in resolving moral and ethical disagreements, resulting in unexpected financial expenses on litigation, loss of brand image, and customer loyalty[6], all because of the lack of a standardised approach to conflict resolution.

Embedding Corporate Social Responsibility in businesses' day-to-day activities focuses on contributing to society's social, economic and ethical well-being[7]. By setting ethical objectives in the framework of building a CSR document, SUR will be able to build up customer loyalty and create a good reputation while keeping its authentic character. Consequently, this essay aims to determine whether introducing a CSR document will financially and ethically benefit the company.

126

Methodology

Business ethics are principles that guide decision-making[8]. Generally, ethics involve analysis of groups' views with different stances. Consequently, in order to holistically analyse the ethical beliefs of various stakeholders of SUR, I will use documents representing the opinions of each group involved in the conflicts: an interview with one of the bar's founders[9] as a primary source, two articles[10][11], a financial statement[12], and an Instagram post[13] as secondary sources.

The interview with the bar's founder will help me gather information about SUR as an organisation, the administration's views on conflicts and the future creation of a CSR document. The articles and an Instagram post will showcase the public and authorities' response to a bar's controversial social media post, accused of racism and inappropriate smoking and drinking areas. Financial documents will be used to estimate the economic aspect of establishing a CSR.

To comprehend the various viewpoints regarding these conflicts, I will use qualitative business tools — Stakeholder mapping and Force Field analysis. I will explore the effects of the CSR document and ethics introduction on the company's financial situation using a Decision Tree.

Analysis

Stakeholder mapping

The stakeholders mapping model is a business tool formulated by Johnson and Scholes. It offers a structured approach to categorising stakeholders involved in an initiative[14]. Placing each stakeholder group of SUR in the matrix will help prioritise engagement efforts, manage risks, and tailor ethical communication — the introduction of the CSR document in particular.

One main weakness of this tool is its inability to deal with the dynamism of stakeholder behaviour. Stakeholders are not static and can become more or less interested in a business because of changes in their personal or professional situation, market conditions or social and ethical norms.

Degree of power		Level of interest	
		Low	High
	Low	Group A: minimal effort Suppliers Bank Local community *(neighbours, kindergarten, inhabitants of the city centre, owners of car transport)* Prospective customers *(online followers)* Media	Group B: keep informed Customers *(teenagers, youths, adults)* Tax office Competitors ('Blanc', 'Gornist', 'Tkemali', '∅36 Kebab')
	High	Group C: keep satisfied Government *(Court, Consumer protection agency, Sanitary inspection)*	Group D: key players Owners (3) Head of the Kitchen *(Chef)* Service manager Waiters Cooks Barista Cleaners

		Level of interest	
Degree of power		Low	High
	Low	Group A: minimal effort Suppliers Bank Media	Group B: keep informed Tax office Competitors ('Blanc', 'Gornist', 'Tkemali', '∅36 Kebab')
	High	Group C: keep satisfied Government *(Court, Consumer protection agency, Sanitary inspection)* Local community *(neighbours, kindergarten, inhibitors of the city centre, owners of car transport)* Prospective customers *(online followers)*	Group D: key players Owners (3) Head of the Kitchen *(Chef)* Service manager Waiters Cooks Barista Cleaners Customers *(teenagers, youths, adults)*

Table 2. Stakeholders map that represent my recommended position of stakeholders considering their interest level and power degree

To create a CSR document, SUR will have to transform from autocratic prioritisation of stakeholder groups into a democratic one. To follow the ideology of the bar[16] and increase its work ethic, SUR needs to move the local community and prospective customers from Group A to C on the map. This approach will not only help to improve bad relationships[17] but also increase brand trust and attract new customers. Placing bar customers into Group D will help to balance the roles in creating a satisfactory CSR document for the most critical stakeholder groups. Given that the ethical impropriety of the bar displeases their regular customers[18], this transformation will be particularly useful in retaining the customer base.

On the contrary, sharing power over decision-making among employees will be disrupted by the high level of customer authority, raising the risk of demotivation among SUR employees. To overcome this problem, the administration must delineate the responsibility and decision-making power areas in the CSR document, which can be lengthy and ethically challenging.

---

[16] Supporting document 1
[17] Supporting document 4
[18] Supporting document 3

6

The bar must be receptive to each stakeholder group to reprioritize stakeholder groups when developing CSR effectively. Through the successful use of an ethical lens, SUR will be able to create a conflict resolution system that is aligned with the bar's original vision.

Decision Tree

A decision tree is a planning tool that helps managers analyse the probability of success of different strategic options[19]. Examining financial differences in the cases of CSR introduction and individual conflict resolution will allow for evaluating the impact of strategic choices on SUR's annual net profit and selecting a more financially favourable path. The main disadvantage of this tool is that the actual outcomes may differ as these are only forecasts and predictions. Moreover, by the time the decision is made, the data used in the estimations may be outdated.

I will use estimates and probabilities based on the information from the interview with SUR's founder[20] and financial document[21] to calculate probable outcomes. Relying exclusively on the bar's owner vision in the context of this business tool may lead to high subjectivity of the results, making them less representative of my research.

Option 1	Forecasted costs	Forecasted annual Net Profit if successful Probability: 0.5	Forecasted annual Net Profit if medium successful Probability: 0.3	Forecasted annual Net Profit if not successful Probability: 0.2
Introduction of the CSR document	≈157333₽	12400000₽	10800000₽	6000000₽

Table 3. Demonstration of the first strategic option[22]

130

In order to calculate the approximate cost of launching a CSR, I will use the formula [23]:

$$\frac{\Sigma \, Net \, Profit \, over \, the \, last \, 3 \, years}{3} \times \, 0,02$$

[19] (IBID PRESS, 2014)
[20] Supporting document 1
[21] Supporting document 2
[22] Supporting documents 1 and 2
[23] (The CSR Universe)

$$\frac{12400000+3200000+8000000}{3} \times \, 0,02 \, \approx \, 157333P^{24}$$

Option 2	Forecast Costs	Forecasted annual net profit if successful Probability: 0.7	Forecasted annual net profit if not successful Probability: 0.3
No changes (implement individual approach to conflict management)	133500P	7700000P	2000000P

Table 4. Demonstration of the second strategic option [25]

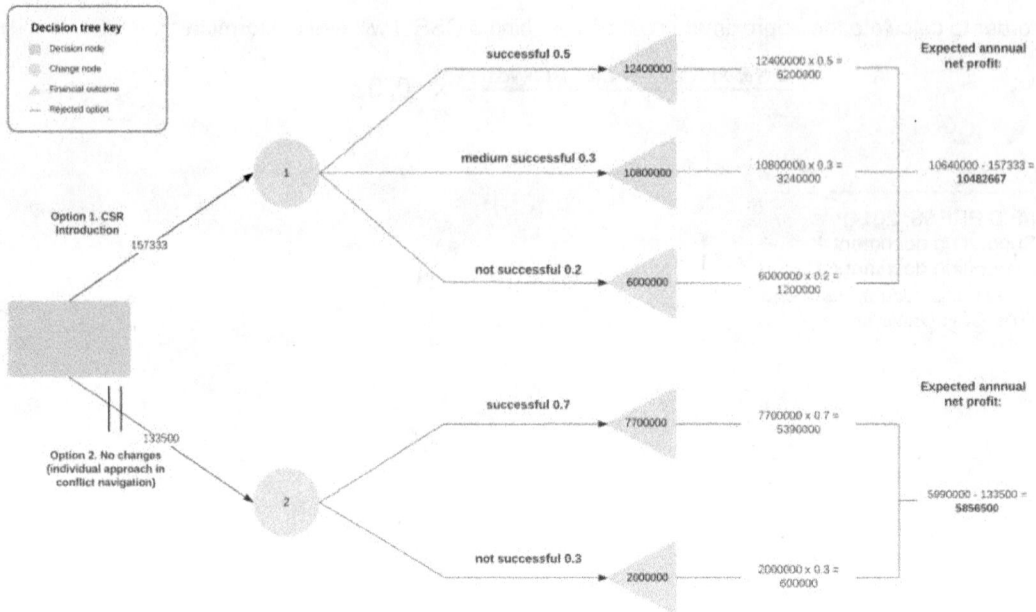

Decision tree key
- Decision node
- Change node
- Financial outcome
- Rejected option

Option 1. CSR Introduction
157333

Option 2. No changes (individual approach in conflict navigation)
133500

successful 0.5 — 12400000 — 12400000 x 0.5 = 6200000

medium successful 0.3 — 10800000 — 10800000 x 0.3 = 3240000

not successful 0.2 — 6000000 — 6000000 x 0.2 = 1200000

Expected annnual net profit: 10640000 - 157333 = 10482667

successful 0.7 — 7700000 — 7700000 x 0.7 = 5390000

not successful 0.3 — 2000000 — 2000000 x 0.3 = 600000

Expected annnual net profit: 5990000 - 133500 = 5856500

Table 6. Decision tree diagram

It is expected that SUR will achieve a 31.03% annual profitability increment, from **8000000₽**[26] to **10482667₽**, if they introduce a CSR document. Adopting an ethically centred Option 1 could allow SUR to improve its sales forecast[27] and, with a probability of 0.5, return to its highest annual net profit recorded in 2021, - **12400000₽**, indicating a **55%** increment from 2023. Annual income may increase to a lesser extent if it will turn out that the conflict resolution methods are not suitable for all stakeholder groups, but only by a minor proportion of **35%** for the 'medium successful' path and a less significant decrease of **33%** for 'not successful'. Although the first option costs **23833₽** more than the second one, it will be a long-term investment and, unlike Option 2, will not be part of the annual costs of the bar. Thus, at the junction of financial and ethical perspectives, it is advised that the CSR document be introduced as it will improve the company's annual net profit and communication with stakeholders.

However, the exact proportion of the increment in net profit is just a mere estimation from the owner. Moreover, the increase may be lower than estimated due to external factors like increased market concentration and decreased interest in SUR[28].

The expected values can only be achieved if SUR develops the CSR as soon as possible to keep up with market interests. Thus, increasing business's profitability will depend on how quickly and efficiently SUR formulates an ethical code of practice in the CSR document.

Lewin's Force Field analysis

Force Field analysis is a tool for analysing the profitability of a company's change by evaluating forces for and against it[29]. Every factor has been rated from 1 to 5 in terms of the impact after the introduction of the CSR document. By calculating the total scores of each section, we can determine whether the decision to introduce CSR will have a positive or negative effect on the relationship between SUR's stakeholder groups.

FFA is criticised for its high level of subjectivity in decision-making. In my case, the use of the analytical tool will be based on the opinion of the bar owner and my own; accordingly, the risks of subjectivity will be quite high.

---

[26] Supporting document 2
[27] Supporting document 1
[28] Supporting document 1
[29] (IBID PRESS, 2014)

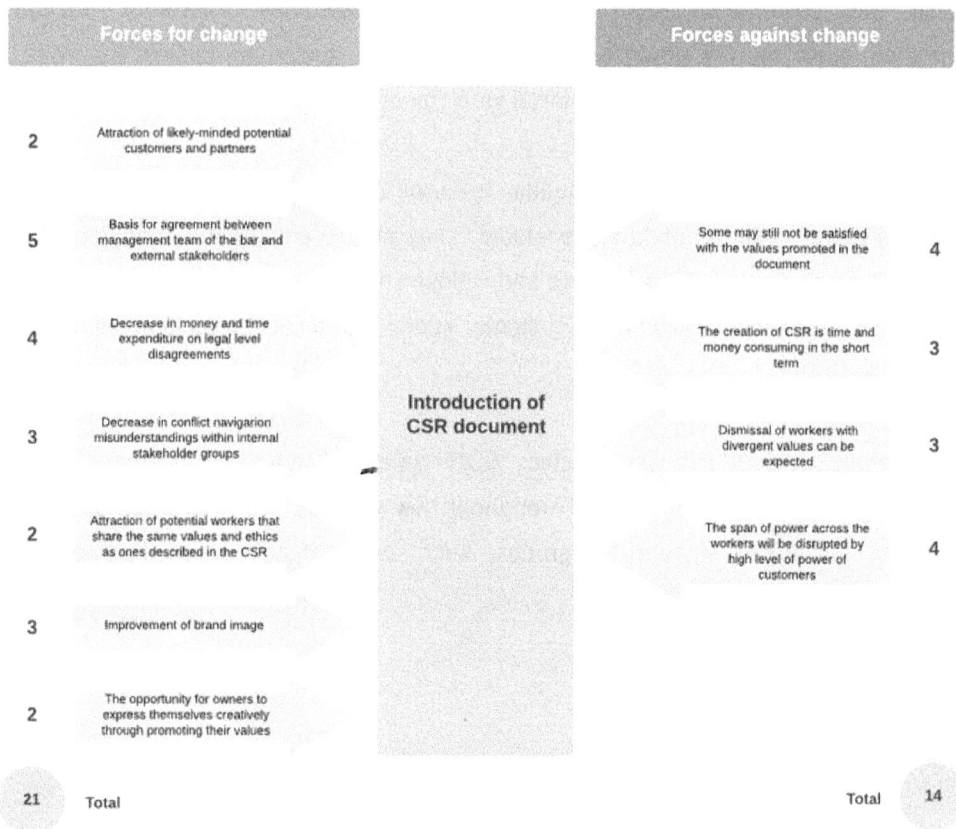

Forces for change		Introduction of CSR document	Forces against change	
2	Attraction of likely-minded potential customers and partners			
5	Basis for agreement between management team of the bar and external stakeholders		Some may still not be satisfied with the values promoted in the document	4
4	Decrease in money and time expenditure on legal level disagreements		The creation of CSR is time and money consuming in the short term	3
3	Decrease in conflict navigation misunderstandings within internal stakeholder groups		Dismissal of workers with divergent values can be expected	3
2	Attraction of potential workers that share the same values and ethics as ones described in the CSR		The span of power across the workers will be disrupted by high level of power of customers	4
3	Improvement of brand image			
2	The opportunity for owners to express themselves creatively through promoting their values			
21	Total		Total	14

Figure 1. Force field diagram representing driving and restricting forces of the implementation of CSR document

133

The analysis indicates that the driving forces quantitatively outweigh the restraining ones. On the positive side, CSR will facilitate conflict resolution, improve company's ethical behaviour, and reduce the amount of money and time spent on litigation[30]. This factor's importance lies in the company's decreased net profit between 2021 and 2022[31]. Implementing CSR objectives can address unforeseen litigation expenses and loss of customer base due to ethical disagreements.

However, the newly developed ethical code of practice, setting up strict limitations on joking and partying freely[32], may dissatisfy some of SUR's loyal customers with values different from what the CSR documents will possess[33]. Striving to satisfy both the local and online

---

[30] Supporting document 1
[31] Supporting document 2
[32] Supporting document 5 and 4
[33] Supporting document 1

10

community and customers, they might face ethical dilemmas. Therefore, the bar's administration must narrow down or redefine its target audience, raising the risks of decreased profits and deviation from the initial ideology of SUR.

To address these concerns, SUR needs to consider the ethical implications and communicate equally with all of its stakeholders. They should explain the changes that the document will entail, especially its fairness and inclusiveness. It's important for SUR to listen to stakeholders' feedback, provide good customer support, and take steps to maintain public trust.

Through carefully considering business ethics, SUR can establish a CSR document, improve its brand image, and act responsibly. Throughout this process, it's crucial for SUR to be responsive to concerned stakeholder groups, such as residents, online followers, and customers[34] .

community and customers, they might face ethical dilemmas. Therefore, the bar's administration must narrow down or redefine its target audience, raising the risks of decreased profits and deviation from the initial ideology of SUR.

To address these concerns, SUR needs to consider the ethical implications and communicate equally with all of its stakeholders. They should explain the changes that the document will entail, especially its fairness and inclusiveness. It's important for SUR to listen to stakeholders' feedback, provide good customer support, and take steps to maintain public trust.

Through carefully considering business ethics, SUR can establish a CSR document, improve its brand image, and act responsibly. Throughout this process, it's crucial for SUR to be responsive to concerned stakeholder groups, such as residents, online followers, and customers[34] .

community and customers, they might face ethical dilemmas. Therefore, the bar's administration must narrow down or redefine its target audience, raising the risks of decreased profits and deviation from the initial ideology of SUR.

To address these concerns, SUR needs to consider the ethical implications and communicate equally with all of its stakeholders. They should explain the changes that the document will entail, especially its fairness and inclusiveness. It's important for SUR to listen to stakeholders' feedback, provide good customer support, and take steps to maintain public trust.

Through carefully considering business ethics, SUR can establish a CSR document, improve its brand image, and act responsibly. Throughout this process, it's crucial for SUR to be responsive to concerned stakeholder groups, such as residents, online followers, and customers[34] .

BIBLIOGRAPHY + APPENDICES OMITTED